CHÖD PRACTICE IN THE BÖN TRADITION

Chöd Practice *in the* Bön Tradition

Tracing the origins of chöd (gcod)
in the Bön tradition,
a dialogic approach cutting
through sectarian boundaries

Alejandro Chaoul

Forewords by Yongdzin Lopon Tenzin Namdak
and Tenzin Wangyal Rinpoche

SNOW LION

BOSTON & LONDON

Snow Lion
An imprint of Shambhala Publications, Inc.
Horticultural Hall
300 Massachusetts Avenue
Boston, Massachusetts 02115
www.shambhala.com

Printed in the United States of America

⊗ This edition is printed on acid-free paper that meets the American
National Standards Institute z39.48 Standard.
♻ Shambhala Publications makes every effort to print on recycled paper.
For more information please visit www.shambhala.com.
Distributed in the United States by Random House, Inc., and in Canada
by Random House of Canada Ltd

Designed and typeset by Gopa & Ted2, Inc.

Library of Congress Cataloging-in-Publication Data
Chaoul, Alejandro.
Chöd practice in the Bön tradition / Alejandro Chaoul;
forewords by Yongdzin Lopon Tenzin Namdak and Tenzin Wangyal.
p. cm.
Includes bibliographical references.
ISBN 978-1-55939-292-1 (alk. paper)
1. Gcod (Bon rite) I. Wangyal, Tenzin. II. Title.
BQ7982.3.C43 2009
299.5'4—dc22
2009008417

If you feel like going to a cemetery, fine, but this is not necessary. A cemetery is a place where corpses and frightening and repulsive things are found. Milarepa said that we permanently have a corpse at our disposal, it is our body! There is even another cemetery, the greatest of all cemeteries, it is the place where all our thoughts and emotions come to die.

— Kalu Rinpoche, *Secret Buddhism: Vajrayāna Practices*

In memory of my first personal teacher,
Ven. Yeshe Dorje Rinpoche,

In gratitude to my parents,
Susi Reich, and Fred Chaoul,

and

With unbounded love for my family:
Erika, Matías & Karina

Table of Contents

Foreword by
Yongdzin Lopon Tenzin Namdak

IN THE BÖN TRADITION, all practices, regardless of whether they pertain to Sutra, Tantra, or Dzogchen, lead one towards the path of liberation. Chöd, however, is a special method with particular characteristics for this. Although Chöd is common to both Tibetan Bön and Buddhist schools, the original basis of this practice in the two traditions is quite different. The Chöd practice according to Buddhist tradition is said to be originally based on the Prajñāpāramitā while that of Tibetan Bön rests upon Tantric practices. However, in both traditions the Chöd practice is performed in a manner which has more in common with Tantra than Sutra, and in both traditions it is known as a very effective and powerful practice bringing the practitioner a strong experience of profound generosity as well as liberation from self-grasping, the root of Samsara. It is, then, a forceful tool for developing one's practice and as such, makes up one of the Four Generosities of the Bön tradition which are practiced on a daily basis.

This book, *The Chöd Practice in the Bön Tradition*, is a first of its kind, attempting a comparison between the Chöd practices of Bön and the Buddhist traditions. Alejandro Chaoul is a long-term student of both academic and spiritual ways, and his thorough examination of both original as well as scholarly sources relating to this practice in Tibetan and in English has resulted in this book. I therefore convey my congratulations to the author for his inspired work and hope this book will be of great benefit for scholars and practitioners alike to widen and enhance their knowledge about this method of practice.

Yongdzin Lopon Tenzin Namdak
Triten Norbutse Monastery
Kathmandu
December 27, 2007

Foreword by
Tenzin Wangyal Rinpoche

ALEJANDRO CHAOUL has been my student for more than fifteen years. Over the years I have known him, he has fully engaged in Bön study and practice, both academically and experientially, and has played an important role in establishing the international activities of Ligmincha Institute through teaching, creating support materials for practice and study, and otherwise offering his dedicated assistance. Besides working with me in his research into the chöd practice, he conducted part of these studies at Tritan Norbutse Monastery in Nepal in close collaboration with my beloved teacher Yongdzin Tenzin Namdak Rinpoche. For all these reasons Chaoul has the ideal level of knowledge and experience necessary for creating this in-depth yet accessible presentation of chöd.

The chöd practice of Bön is very much rooted in many of the teachings of the Bön tradition, such as the Mother Tantra (*Ma Gyü*), as Chaoul rightly points out. Chöd continues to be widely practiced in the East, and since its recent introduction to the West, it has been met with much enthusiasm by Western students in the Bön Buddhist communities.

Chaoul's book offers a comprehensive intellectual understanding of chöd and its origins within both the Bön and Buddhist traditions, and as such will have great benefit for scholars as well as for those who wish to engage in chöd as a daily ritual or meditation practice.

As Chaoul concludes, the similarities between the Bön and Buddhist forms of the practice are more valid than their differences. The core purpose of chöd is to turn fear into a path to liberation. The practitioner actively seeks out fearful experiences, using fear as an opportunity to visualize cutting apart one's own physical body, symbolizing the cutting of the ego, and thus cultivating wisdom. The practitioner further visualizes transforming the body into an offering that satisfies all beings, thus cultivating generosity and detachment.

Through this ancient and profound practice, anyone who is able to recognize their own fear — whether its source is external or internal — can face that fear, challenge it, and overcome it. Ultimately, fear becomes a tool to cultivate enlightened qualities. Anyone who understands these principles of the chöd practice will be benefited, and this book offers an excellent contribution to this understanding.

— Geshe Tenzin Wangyal Rinpoche

Acknowledgments

THE LACK OF INFORMATION on the Bön tradition of chöd (*gcod*), inspiration from Ven. Yeshe Dorje Rinpoche and Namkhai Norbu Rinpoche concerning the topic and practice of chöd, and my particular deep interest in the Bön tradition as a whole led me to explore chöd and its origins in the Bön tradition. In this enterprise the help provided by Yongdzin Tenzin Namdak Rinpoche[1] and Tenzin Wangyal Rinpoche has been invaluable to the point that no words in either English or Tibetan suffice to express my most sincere thanks and *thug je che* (*thugs rje che*).

This book stems from my MA thesis at the University of Virginia. I would like to thank my advisors, David Germano and Karen Lang, for their suggestions and encouragement, and in particular, David Germano, whose commitment to excellence and continuous support are a great source of inspiration. Thanks also are due to the Rocky Foundation for awarding me a Buddhist Fellowship that allowed me to visit Yongdzin Tenzin Namdak in Nepal, whose help, as I mentioned, was invaluable for this project.

The translation of the chöd sādhana, *Laughter of the Skygoers* (*mKha' 'gro'i gad rgyang*), was done in close consultation with Yongdzin Tenzin Namdak Rinpoche and Tenzin Wangyal Rinpoche. Later revisions were also done with the Ligmincha Institute translation team, of which I am a member.

I owe Geshe Lungrig Namgyal a special thanks for creating an index of the *Secret Mother Tantra* (*Ma rgyud*) chöd text on my behalf. Nawang Thokmey, librarian of the Tibetan collection at the University of Virginia, has been very helpful in helping me to find different Tibetan texts, and so was Lopon (now Khenpo) Tenpa'i Yungdrung from Tritsan Norbutse Monastery in Kathmandu, Nepal. Andrea Frolic, Sheldon Smart, and Cindy Loew were proofreaders of great aid in the first incarnation of this project; they had the hard task of helping my prose flow better in English. Even my mother-in-law, Katy Chamberlain, helped me beautify this book, by drawing one of the figures, the Bönpo bell. When I was writing my MA thesis, Dan Martin helpfully reviewed some of my speculations. My participation in the recent panel at the IATS (International Association of Tibetan Studies) in Bonn, Germany, organized by Giacomella Orofino, brought a much-needed "re-touch." I appreciate the insights and criticisms offered during the panel and outside of it by Dan Martin, Donatella Rossi, and Giacomella Orofino; they gave me an opportunity to refine some points that otherwise would have been left unclear or stated inaccurately.[2] Personal and e-mail discussions with Geoffrey Samuel, especially regarding the theoretical contextualization of chöd in Tibetan societies, added nuance and precision to my proposed framework. His generous availability and constructive criticism have characterized a cherished relationship of distance mentorship. Words cannot express enough my appreciation for his continuous collegiality and honesty over the years. I also want to thank my friend Mark Dahlby for his very valuable editing of this work in its transition from MA thesis to book, and my friend John Jackson who provided great help by digitizing many of the images used in this book, including the cover photo.

The acknowledgments would not be complete without thanking Jeff Cox and Sidney Piburn, of Snow Lion Publications, who gave me the support and motivation to bring my work into book form, and Liz Green and Michael Wakoff, also of Snow Lion Publications, who provided great insights during the editing process and helped me complete the book. In fact, working with Michael the last two months made me realize that the "devil is in the details." I can't thank him enough for helping me "cut through" so many of those and making this book so much better.

Finally, I would like to thank my wife, Erika de la Garza, who has constantly supported this project, despite the nights without sleep. Her help in proofreading, making suggestions, and accompanying me to Nepal added a special perspective to this study. At the time I was completing my thesis, our first child, Matías Namdak, was born; now we also have a wonderful girl, Karina Dawa. To them I owe the everyday lessons of cutting through anger and attachment in trying to realize some glimpses of wisdom and unconditional love. My unconditional gratitude goes to all three.

Technical Note

THROUGHOUT this work my practice is to phoneticize Tibetan names and include their transliteration, italicized and in parenthesis, at their first occurrence. The transliteration follows the system devised by Turrell Wylie (see "A Standard System of Tibetan Transcription," *Harvard Journal of Asiatic Studies* 22 [1959]: 261–67), with the modification that the first pronounced letter is capitalized, as in Jeffrey Hopkins, *Meditation on Emptiness* (London: Wisdom Publications, 1983). For names of deities which are repeated, I also include their translation, in quotation marks, in the same parenthesis as the transliteration, at their first occurrence, but continue citing them by their phoneticized name.

Technical expressions and relevant Tibetan words are introduced in the body of the text in their English translation, with their transliteration, also italicized and in parenthesis, at their first occurrence. For these, no letters are capitalized. When Tibetan and Sanskrit are given, both are italicized in parenthesis with the Tibetan first. Where the context requires it, I repeat the transliteration of a crucial word.

A few Sanskrit terms that are part of common Buddhist parlance are treated as English words, but with diacritics where pertinent (e.g., "Buddha," "Mahāyāna," "tantra," "sādhana").

As for terms which are phoneticized differently by various authors cited, I provide my usage in brackets at the first occurrence, for example, chö [chöd], Bon [Bön], and for their transliterations, I either provide my usage in brackets at its first occurrence or modify them and mention the modification in the corresponding footnote.

I use the male gender, but provide the male and female gender at their first occurrence to make clear that both are included.

Introduction: Enchanted by the Melody

IT BEGAN during the beautiful Fall season of 1989 in Zil-non Kagye Ling (*Zil gnon bka' brgyad gling*) Monastery in Dharamsala, India. On a clear moonlit night, I first heard the melody that transformed my life. A striking voice accompanied by powerful bells and drums reached my small room not too far from the lama's house. Although I was eager to come down and see where it was coming from, I stayed tucked in my slim mattress, rocked by the enchanting melody, not even worried by the spider and the mouse that usually roamed in my room.

The next morning I asked Karma Sonam, the lama's son, what that melody was, and he told me it was a tape of the ritual of chöd (*gcod*, lit. "cutting") sung by his father, Ngakpa Yeshe Dorje Rinpoche, who at that time was teaching in the United States. That sensual melody and its rhythmic, rapid drumming captivated me. Just like Pavlov's dog, every time I heard it, my mind "salivated" with curiosity.

Dharamsala is a small village in the north of India, the site of His Holiness the Dalai Lama's Tibetan government in exile, where a few thousand Tibetan people have settled. This was my first trip to India, and among the various fascinating places I had visited, Dharamsala felt like home. Not that it had any similarity to the large urban environment of my native Buenos Aires, but, inexplicably, it felt like an inner home.

Studying at Dharamsala's Library of Tibetan Works and Archives (LTWA), I learned more about Buddhism in general. I was also able to visit monasteries of the four different Tibetan traditions, Nyingma, Kagyu, Sakya, and Gelug, and learn more about these traditions. Zilnon Kagye Ling was Nyingma, the most "ancient" among the four, but at LTWA they taught mostly from the Gelugpa perspective, the most prevalent tradition and the one closely associated with the Tibetan government in exile. Bön was seldom mentioned.

A ngakpa (*sngags pa*, yogi or tantric practitioner) named Karma Lhundrup, who was doing the classic three-year retreat at Zilnon Kagye Ling, became my spiritual friend (*dge' ba'i grogs pa*) and slowly taught me some mantras, rituals, breathing exercises, the preliminary practices (*sngon 'gro*), and a little more about chöd, especially from the Nyingma perspective.

Some months later Yeshe Dorje Rinpoche came back from the United States, and I was able to meet him on Losar (*lo gsar*), the Tibetan New Year—which was in late February through the beginning of March 1990. At four o' clock in the morning, after a ritual in the temple or *gompa* (*dgon pa*) welcoming the new year, I was invited to Rinpoche's house. There I joined a small group of family and ngakpas around a table talking, joking, and eating *chango* (*chang sngo*)— a mixture of fermented rice, barley, raisins, and other ingredients served hot in a cup with strips of dry meat on top. Yeshe Dorje Rinpoche was a wonderful ngakpa who had visited 108 charnel grounds in Tibet practicing chöd, before escaping to India, there becoming His Holiness the Dalai Lama's "weather man" and establishing Zilnon Kagye Ling. He had an intriguing presence, with a long white moustache and his hair tied in a knot on top of his head holding a small oval metal case. His smile was broad and contagious, and his presence felt powerful and cozy at the same time. I was clearly at home.

In the next few months, I helped at the monastery in various ways, from building walls and painting to carrying the offerings during the rituals. I would continue to meet with Karma Lhundrup, and I saw Yeshe Dorje Rinpoche, but because of my inability to speak Tibetan and his inability to speak English, our communication was limited to hand gestures and smiles, which I enjoyed immensely. From Karma Lhundrup I learnt that Tromo (*khro mo*), also known as Black Vajrayogini, was the main deity of Rinpoche's chöd practice. This alerted me to the realization that there was more than one chöd. Yeshe Dorje Rinpoche was well known for his connection with Tromo, and many practitioners sought to receive the Tromo initiation from him. Someone formally requested Rinpoche to give this initiation, which included the initiation into its chöd practice, and I got word that Rinpoche wanted me to be there. It was an unfamiliar honor for me, and although I was trying to focus on the ritual itself, I was also drawn to look around and see the other lamas, monks, ngakpas, local Tibetans, and some tourists/practitioners like myself. When this incredible spiritual spectacle concluded and we were outside, Rinpoche stared at me, moving his hand as if he still had his damaru (*da ma ru*)[3] and laughed loudly in his usual manner. His son, Karma Sonam, told me that this meant that eventually I ought to do this practice as well.

I learned some more before the trip ended and was given an English text of the preliminaries, which also included a brief explanation about chöd; a brief English text of Tromo and her chöd; and a copy of the tape I had originally heard that memorable evening almost six months before. I took all these back to Argentina, where I enthusiastically practiced and studied daily. Over the years, I had the opportunity to travel again to India, Nepal, and the United States, where I learned from various lamas of different traditions, especially from the Dzogchen master Namkhai Norbu Rinpoche and the Bön Dzogchen masters Yongdzin Tenzin Namdak and Tenzin Wangyal Rinpoche. Always trying to deepen my understanding of this fascinating practice, I learned several different traditions of chöd, mostly from among the Nyingma and Bön lineages. I also noticed that many practitioners, especially in Argentina and Mexico, but also in the United States, were attracted to chöd for its instruments and melody as well as for the radical idea of severing one's ego.

Wanting to understand more about the philosophical-religious background of the practices that so profoundly engaged me and to study these traditions from an academic viewpoint, I enrolled in a master's program in religious studies at the University of Virginia. Needless to say, when the time to choose a master's thesis topic arrived, I selected chöd. I also quickly realized that there was a lack of information on the Bön tradition of chöd, both in the scholarly field as well as among practitioners and the general public. This, combined with the inspiration from Yeshe Dorje Rinpoche, Namkhai Norbu Rinpoche, and Tenzin Wangyal Rinpoche concerning the practice of chöd, and my growing interest in the Bön tradition as a whole, led me to explore the intriguing practice of chöd and its origins in the Bön tradition.

In tracing the history of chöd in the Bön tradition, I found myself entangled exploring the possible interrelations of the chöd practice in both Bön and Buddhism and, to some extent, trying to determine "which came first." In this study, I aim to bring a "dialogical" awareness—borrowing Mikhail Bakhtin's term—to the chöd practice, which will illuminate chöd as an example of the interplay between Tibetan cultural practices in general and their reinterpretation and recontextualization by Buddhist scholastic schemes.[4] Bakhtin, a Russian linguist and literary critic, approaches texts and practices "dialogically." Instead of treating a text or practice monologically as a linear, self-contained unit (i.e., like a monologue), Bakhtin treats it as in constant *dialogue* with other texts, literary works, authors, practices, and even contexts. It is thus a more expansive and inclusive approach, continuously informed by, and in communication with, multiple "others," where various approaches can coexist.

In this book, I will be using Bakhtin's dialogical approach in the simplified manner that Stan Mumford does in *Himalayan Dialogue*, where he describes three stages in a dialogical process: "ancient matrix," "individual life sequence" of a new directional identity, and "historical becoming" that unites both.[5] Using Bakhtin via Mumford in this way will serve as a functional lens that can help us see earlier strata of significance of the chöd practice and the way these were historically transformed, without having to adhere to one single form or label. I believe that the beauty of this rich, intricate, and often misunderstood practice, is to be found in the coexistence of many different views, which can expand beyond the traditional horizons delimited by social, academic, and sectarian boundaries. This, I will argue, is part and parcel of what the chöd practice itself facilitates.

Chöd: Offering One's Body

 CHÖD IS a meditative practice that is not performed while sitting quietly and comfortably on a cushion inside a shrine room, but instead is purposely practiced in frightening places, such as cemeteries and charnel grounds. This brings a feeling of fear that is then used by the chöpa (*gcod pa*, chöd practitioner) to cut his or her own ego. Singing, dancing, and playing special bone instruments, the chöd practitioner visualizes the dismemberment, cooking, and finally the offering of his own body as part of a banquet for an assembly of enlightened and unenlightened beings, such as protectors and all kinds of sentient beings. Even demons and spirits are invited and fed! In this energetic and physically active practice, the chöpa's attire and implements add to the way the practice is internalized by the practitioner. Traditionally, the chöpa is dressed in animal skins and uses real bone instruments, animal and human, such as the thighbone trumpet (*rkang gling*). The photo on the cover depicts such a chöpa in the eastern Tibetan region of Kham. The frightening environment and attire enhance the feeling of fear in the practitioner, and it is precisely that feeling and the attachment to the body that is "cut" as one visualizes cutting and offering one's body. The Tibetan lama, scholar, and chöd master, Namkhai Norbu Rinpoche, states: "By summoning up what is most dreaded, and openly offering what we usually most want to protect, the *chöd* works to cut us out of the double bind of the ego and attachment to the body."[6]

BASIC ELEMENTS OF THE CHÖD PRACTICE

What follows could be understood as a generic template common to all chöd traditions. Once the chöpa is well trained in a peaceful site, he is ready to perform the practice in a terrifying environment. The "mystic drama, performed by a single human actor, assisted by numerous spiritual beings, visualized, or imagined, as being present in response to his magic invocation,"[7] then begins. Blowing the thighbone trumpet, he calls all the spirits to invite them to the feast, and with the aid of the drum and bell, the chöpa abides in the state of the nonduality of emptiness and appearance. In this meditative state, he expels his consciousness from his body, the consciousness becoming a deity, usually a female one (Tib. *mkha' 'gro*, Skt. *ḍākinī*) and the body a corpse from which the guests will feast.[8] The deity severs the cranium and then chops the corpse in pieces, placing the flesh, blood, and bones inside the cranium, which becomes a cauldron. With a low fire, the flesh, blood, and bones become nectar which satisfies all the desires of the enlightened and nonenlightened guests.[9] No one is to be excluded, and that is why after this offering—usually called a "white feast"—a "red feast" of just raw flesh, blood, and bones is offered for the more "carnivorous" guests in a manner reminiscent both of animal sacrifices and the Tibetan custom of "sky burial," in which a corpse is chopped up for consumption by vultures (see figure 1).[10]

FIGURE 1. Vultures at a sky burial, Tibet. Photo by Tenzin Wangyal Rinpoche.

These offerings are endless in that they suffice no matter how many guests come or how big their appetite is, and are infinite in that they transform into whatever the guests desire. At the end, the chöpa feels that all the desires of every guest have been thoroughly satisfied, in both quantity and quality, and that everything one has to offer has been given: "psychic liberation is fused with ethical indebtedness."[11] In other words, the chöpa seeks not just self-liberation, but to liberate all sentient beings (i.e., the altruistic bodhichitta intent).

This highly sensorial practice is based on religious texts that are found mostly in the Nyingma, Kagyu, and Bön traditions of Tibet, yet Western scholars have largely overlooked this practice. Interestingly, even among Tibetans its status is ambiguous. On one hand, many chöpas can be seen along the market streets or pilgrimage roads performing this ritual to get some money, and yet on the other hand, it is not a widely taught or "mainstream" practice. Ngakpas (and some monks too, but fewer) also perform chöd when on pilgrimage, both as a way to dispel obstacles along their journey and earn some money. Tibetans, attracted by the melody and knowing about the ritual, will give a few coins to the chöpas, in much the same way as passersby donate money to artistic street-performers in Euro-American countries. Many times the ritual is performed to cure illnesses, stop hailstorms, and so forth, in the belief that, as Snellgrove writes, "enemies, adverse influences and hindrances are released as the circle of offerings"[12] becomes purified. The famous *Blue Annals* has accounts of chöpas who cured lepers, created or stopped storms, and healed their own illnesses such as tuberculosis, and it even reports that "many who were blind and deaf were cured on the spot."[13] However, many people nowadays believe that some of these people are not real practitioners but just "performers" who have learnt (and sometimes not even that well) the external part of the ritual of singing and playing the drum and bell. Furthermore, not only are these performers thought to be misrepresenting the purpose of the practice, but it is even more upsetting that they are asking for money for such performances.

Although chöd appears in some monastic curricula in the Bön tradition, it is only for a very few who follow more of a meditation curriculum, whereas the mainstream monastic school attendees are not even allowed to play the drum, except in prayer gatherings, which never include the practice of chöd.[14]

Therefore, to a certain extent, chöd still remains a marginal, yet intriguing practice for both native Tibetan communities and Western scholars. My interest is thus to explore the way in which this "funky" and intriguing practice can be considered to be a religious and spiritual pursuit.[15]

WESTERN SCHOLARSHIP
ON CHÖD IN THE BÖN TRADITION

A little over a decade ago, in his *Machig Labdrön and the Foundations of Chöd* , Jerome Edou wrote:

> Strangely enough, amid the profusion of scholarly works on Tibetan Buddhism, not a single in-depth study devoted to the Chöd tradition has been published, with the exception of an excellent article by Janet Gyatso. The majority of Western researchers have contented themselves with approximate accounts, often reducing the entire system to the offering of one's body to the demons, the most spectacular aspect of the rite.[16]

The article Edou refers to is Gyatso's "The Development of the *Gcod* Tradition,"[17] although in a footnote he also mentions the unpublished dissertation by Carol Savvas, "A Study of the Profound Path of Gcod,"as well as some references which either briefly mention the practice of chöd or translate certain ritual documents of the practice.[18] Edou reasserts that Gyatso's article "is the only serious study published so far," and therefore the one that "has been the starting point" for his own study.[19]

Since then, a few more books have come out.[20] However, all of these works focus on the lineage originating with Machig Labdrön (*Ma gcig lab sgron*) and Padampa Sangye (*Pha dam pa sangs rgyas*). Some of these authors mention the possibility of finding this practice also within the Bön tradition, but no one has done any extensive research in this area; most merely mention some of the names and broad classifications of Bön chöd texts.[21] The recent IATS panel, "Origin and Developments of the Zhi byed and gCod Traditions in the Cultural History of Tibet," presented one of the most interesting arrays of scholarly work on this topic, which, I believe, is a reflection of a growing interest on the part of Tibetan Buddhist practitioners and scholars.[22]

In her "landmark" article, Janet Gyatso mentions the classifications of Bön chöd texts "into four types corresponding to the four tantric activities: peaceful, extending, powerful, and wrathful."[23] She lists some chöd texts from the Bön tradition in her footnotes[24] and asserts that even though time did not permit her to investigate this more, "perhaps these texts can shed light on the development of Gcod as a whole."[25] Namkhai Norbu Rinpoche mentions and directs us to Samten Karmay's *Catalogue of Bonpo Publications*, which refers only to the *Cycle of the Secret Skygoers (mKha' 'gro gsang gcod rgyud skor)* and the *Essential Advice on the Profound Chöd (Zab mo gcod kyi gdams ngag)*.[26] Edou's study mostly restates Janet Gyatso's remarks regarding the chöd in the Bön tradition and lists in his bibliography only four of the six Bön chöd texts that Gyatso mentions (though he adds more detailed information on them). However in his brief remarks on the chöd in the Bön tradition, Edou makes several important points:

> Finally, the Bön tradition as well possesses its Chöd cycles, some of them coming from the hearing transmission (*snyan rgyud*), others from the Recovered Treasure traditions [*gter ma*], but Machig does not appear in any of lineages of these two traditions. According to [Yongdzin] Tenzin Namdak, all the Bön traditions of Chöd follow the highest tantras."[27]

Note that Edou acknowledges that the Bön tradition possesses its own chöd cycles and that he stresses their differentiation from Machig's lineage. He emphasizes this difference by highlighting the association of the Bön chöd with the highest tantras, while affirming that Machig's chöd is based on the *Perfection of Insight Sūtra* (Tib. *Shes rab kyi pha rol tu phyin pa*, Skt. *Prajñāpāramitā*).[28]

John Reynolds, a scholar whose work focuses primarily on translations of Bön teachings, has completed a translation of the *Laughter of the Ḍākinīs (mKha' 'gro'i gad rgyang)*, a Bön chöd sādhana from the nineteenth century—of which my translation is included in appendix 1—but he does not investigate the evolution of chöd within the Bön tradition. However, in his preface to that translation, Reynolds provides a brief introduction to the topic of chöd, which includes Buddhist and Bön sources. Among the Bön sources, he states that chöd is included in the *Ninefold Preliminary Prac-*

tices (*sngon 'gro*) from the *Experiential Transmission of Zhang Zhung* (*Zhang zhung nyams rgyud*), in *Gyalwa's Instruction Manual* (*rGyal ba phyag khrid*) of Druchen Gyalwa Yungdrung (*Bru chen rgyal ba gyung drung*, 1242–90);[29] in the "Fearful Place" (*gnyan sa lam*) chapter, which is among the six practices of the path of the *Mother Tantra Cycle* (*Ma rgyud skor*); and in newer texts from visionary transmissions and the New Bön tradition (*gsar bon*).[30] Reynolds concludes his report affirming that "the history of the development of Chod in the Bon tradition has yet to be written."[31] Annette Jones has translated a fourteenth-century chöd text from the Bön tradition, but did not investigate the Bön chöd tradition as a whole.[32] And Donatella Rossi has presented a wonderful study on the "Chöd of the Secret Skygoers" in the IATS conference, and hopefully she will publish her study soon.[33]

Thus we can see that there has been a lack of detailed studies among Euro-American scholars regarding chöd within the Bön tradition. This book remedies that gap by addressing the topic based on the accounts given in the available Tibetan Bön chöd texts, together with oral instructions and remarks by living Bönpo lamas and scholars, chief among them Yongdzin Tenzin Namdak Rinpoche, who is regarded in the Bön tradition as the most knowledgeable scholar and meditator alive today. As for Euro-American material regarding the context of chöd in the Bön tradition, this book will rely primarily on works by Dan Martin and John Reynolds, and, to a lesser extent, on David Snellgrove's *The Nine Ways of Bon*.[34]

Buddhist Perspectives on the Origin of Chöd and the Issue of "Shamanism"

According to Edou, the Tibetan chöd (*bod gcod*) is an articulation of the Indian sūtric teachings of the *Perfection of Insight*, integrated with Tibetan tantric practices, including rediscovered treasures (*gter ma*).[35] Its creation is attributed to the Tibetan female teacher Machig Labdrön (1031–1129 C.E.), who named it the *Chöd of Mahāmudrā* (*Dam cho phyag rgya chen po'i gcod yul*). Based primarily on the *Pacification* [of Suffering] (*zhi byed*) teachings of the eleventh-century Indian Pandit Padampa Sangye, Machig's chöd was "also known as the teaching 'With the Object of Cutting Demons' (*bDud kyi gcod yul*)."[36] Edou appears to overemphasize its source in Indian Buddhism and its being grounded on the philosophical view of the *Perfection of*

Insight Sūtra.[37] He is also concerned to refute those Euro-American scholars who heighten the seemingly "shamanic" aspects of the chöd ritual, for example, visualizing the dismemberment of one's body.[38] Edou considers those accounts sensationalistic "shamanizing interpretations" and instead proposes that "the specific methods of Chöd such as the offering of one's body, . . . seem directly derived from the Bodhisattva tradition, as described in the *Jātaka* stories."[39] Chöd is a meditative practice, but not one modeled overtly on peaceful actions—although not all of the Bodhisattva's stories are peaceful either. For example, for experienced practitioners, chöd is performed in cemeteries and charnel grounds, not for their peaceful nature, but because they can bring fear into the practitioner:[40]

> Practitioners of *Jod* [chöd] are traditionally nomadic, traveling continually from place to place with a minimum of possessions, as mendicants, often carrying nothing more than the ritual instruments of damaru, a bell and a thigh bone trumpet. . . . The practice is principally undertaken in lonely and desolate places, such as caves and mountain peaks, but in particular graveyards and charnel grounds at night, when the terrifying energy of such places serves to intensify the sensation of the practitioner who, seated alone in the dark, summons all those to whom he owes a karmic debt to come and receive payment in the form of the offering of his body. . . . By summoning up what is most dreaded, and openly offering what we usually most want to protect, the *Jod* works to cut us out of the double bind of the ego and attachment to the body. In fact the name *Jod* means 'to cut'; but it is the attachment, not the body itself that is the problem to cut through.[41]

Because of its dreadful and terrifying character, this ritual is sometimes seen as marginal. Some may see that marginality itself as part of shamanism. Geoffrey Samuel, on the other hand, has a more inclusive view of the "shamanic." He contrasts a "shamanic" orientation to a "clerical" orientation, where the shamanic is a cultural modality which preceded the arrival of Buddhism in Tibetan societies, but that was relegated to a background role with the advent of the clerical, monastic institutions in the fourteenth century.[42] Samuel describes the "shamanic" as the regulation and transformation of human life and human society through the use (or purported use) of alternative states of consciousness by means of which specialist practitioners are held to communicate with a mode of reality alternative to, and more fundamental than, the world of everyday experience.[43]

Samuel adds that in this sense, the "shamanic" refers to

a category of practices found in differing degrees in almost all human societies. . . . The term is in no way at all derogatory. In fact, I believe that the sophisticated body of shamanic practices within Tibetan Buddhism probably constitutes Tibet's most important single contribution to humanity.[44]

But Samuel's definition is not accepted by all scholars. Georges Dreyfus criticizes Samuel's usage of the "shamanic" because "his description of the Tibetan tradition as constituted by the opposition of clerical and shamanic elements makes a mockery of any scholarly use of shamanism."[45] Dreyfus appears to limit "shamanism" to folk practitioners in what he calls the "narrow (and more or less proper) sense of the word."[46] Per Kvaerne and others[47] hold an even narrower view, limiting the category to its origins in the Siberian, Tungusic, or Manchu term "*saman*" meaning "priest."[48] Although Kvaerne criticizes Samuel's "shamanic" category as being so broad that almost any meditative practice would fit his definition, it is not the case that, for example, practitioners using the classic meditative practices of "calm abiding" (Tib. *gzhi nas*, Skt. *shamata*) "communicate with a mode of reality alternative to, and more fundamental than, the world of everyday experience."[49] Furthermore, Samuel does not use the term "shamanism" but rather "shamanic," which he explains as an analytic, cross-cultural category that is useful for describing these kinds of modalities as "orientations" in different societies.[50]

Although the term "shamanism" does not have an equivalent in Tibetan, many Tibetan practices and practitioners clearly fit the "shamanic orientation," especially the wide variety of tantric practices, tantric practitioners, and ngakpas. It is also important to understand that a monk or a nun practicing a tantric ritual, for example, would be included in Samuel's category of "shamanic orientation." In fact they would be included among the "civilized shamans" that Samuel discusses in his book of the same title. Looking at Samuel's category via Mumford's three stages of dialogical approach mentioned earlier, Samuel's shamanic orientation corresponds to Mumford's first stage, the ancient matrix. With Buddhism's migration from India to Tibet in the seventh–eighth century, the ancient matrix "in Tibetan societies was constantly under attack, either overtly or implicitly, by Buddhism, but it reconstituted itself. . . . [T]hroughout Tibetan history, it provided a background against which Buddhism took shape and in terms of which it had to justify itself."[51] If Samuel is right that the shamanic orientation of Tibetan society provides the background or matrix in which Tibetan Buddhism developed, then Dreyfus's confinement of the shamanic to folk practitioners makes the category too narrow. It ignores the fact that the indigenous Tibetan folk tradition has been in continual dialogue (as well as quarrel) with the Buddhist teachings from India, as the latter's sophisticated, philosophical, and nonfolk approach was received by the Tibetan culture. As evidence of this mingling of two cultures, Geoffrey Samuel notes: "followers of all five traditions, *Bon po* and Buddhists, take part in shamanic procedures of a less sophisticated kind, those involving spirit-mediums and other folk-religion divinatory techniques, *bsangs* offerings to local deities, and the like."[52] In other words, there was a confluence of the underlying ancient matrix, which by then had already assimilated Bön teachings, and the Buddhist teachings from India.

Although Samuel contrasts the clerical and shamanic orientations in Tibetan culture, they both share the bodhi ideal: the practices and practitioners of both orientations have enlightenment or buddhahood as their aim. Therefore, the topic of chöd makes for a fascinating case study in this context since it intersects not only the categories of the clerical and the shamanic but also the sūtric and tantric.

Chöd is also a very powerful path to buddhahood. Its power comes from working with the practitioner's afflictive emotions. For example, Harding observes that "Chöd is distinctive in its radical methods of intensifying obsession and inducing emotional upheavals and apparitions of fear, the better to observe and sever them."[53] Chöd is purposely performed in frightening places to help the practitioner connect to the gods and demons or god-demons (inner and outer),[54] heightening his fear so that he has the opportunity to cut through it. This fear is used by the chöpa and is expressed in "an energetic and physically active practice,"[55] by singing, dancing, and playing special bone instruments, while visualizing the dismemberment, cooking, and finally the offering of his own body.[56]

CUTTING THROUGH THE MEANING

The etymology of "chöd," besides *gcod*, meaning "cutting," is related to its homonym *spyod*, usually translated as "practice," and thus in particular to the practices of the *Perfection of Insight*.[57] Edou states that Jamgön Kontrul combines both meanings, of "cutting" and "practice" as the "conduct of the bodhisattvas,"[58] thereby creating his own definition of this practice:

> The profound practice (*spyod*) of the Prajñāpāramitā,
> The Chöd (*gcod*) that aims at cutting through demons.[59]

This is what Edou refers to as "the (Chöd) practice (of the bodhisattvas)," (*spyod yul*).[60] Savvas similarly asserts that *spyod* refers to "the practices of the Method and Wisdom [or Insight] in which a follower of the chöd tradition engages to develop the two Bodhicittas (Conventional and Ultimate)."[61] She adds that according to Ven. Geshe Champa Lodro Rinpoche, "the practice of gCod [chöd] is the means of increasing the two Bodhicittas."[62] Savvas also cites Machig Labdrön herself in *The Uncommon Eight Chapters* as pointing to the integration of these two interpretations of the term "chöd":

> So whatever appearances arise, one should *cut* (*gCod*) them off directly (giving up anything which is an obstacle to the Six Perfections) and should *practice* the activities (*spyod pa*) which are meritorious (i.e., the Six Perfections).[63]

Furthermore, Edou believes:

> One should differentiate the generic term "chöd" [*gcod*] as "cutting through the ego and its emotional entanglements (and in this sense would seem as ancient as Buddhism itself), and the

"Chöd" [also *gcod* but as the] doctrine of "cutting through demonic objects" (*bdud kyi gcod yul*), for which Machig was the source and inspiration."[64]

Edou quotes a passage from Machig's *Concise Life Story*, which states that before her, there was no tradition which transformed the aggregates into food offerings to satisfy the gods and demons.[65] And from this he jumps to the conclusion that "even if certain elements of Chöd present lexicographical similarities with certain shamanistic rites, the latter are considered 'erroneous forms of Chöd' (*gcod log*)."[66]

There is no doubt that the chöd practice is deeply influenced philosophically by the *Perfection of Insight* teachings and practice, but I believe that overemphasizing that influence and referring to chöd's tantric aspects only in a sterilized manner leads to a mistaken view of it. Anthropologist Toni Huber observes that explanations of Tibetan pilgrimage practices tend to privilege the "Indic doctrinal explanations for what Tibetans do and say [which] has drawn the analytical focus away from a closer investigation of the assumed *emic* categories."[67] In other words, the Tibetans' own cultural perspective, one that is meaningful to many members of Tibetan society, is distorted by imported Indian values.

Edou and others may be privileging Indic explanations of chöd in a similar fashion. Furthermore, because the use of "shamanistic" is not defined in these works, and the "shamanistic" is just dismissed, their critique falters. There should be no doubt that chöd belongs to Samuel's category of shamanic orientation, or perhaps to a narrower subcategory of it, which we could call "ngakpa orientation." It is also important to remember that in this category, the so-called shamanic and tantric aspects are intertwined, rather than the former being "foul" and the latter "pure." On a similar note, Savvas writes:

> The gcod system is a union of both Sūtra and Tantra, and as such a multivalent approach to the subject has been necessary, for, as scholars such as Edward Conze have noted, tantric traditions have regularly been misrepresented by Western scholars, whose purely philological approach to the texts has proven unsatisfactory due to the highly symbolic and enigmatic style of the material.[68]

Within Tibetan Buddhist mind training, tantra is not just a higher philosophical view than sūtra, but it needs the foul and impure in order to transform them into their pure counterparts. Surely, the complexity of tantric practices, in particular its sexual and seemingly violent aspects, has often been misinterpreted and misunderstood, both in its original context and by Euro-American scholars. A more sterilized interpretation often results, where the meaning is kept, but concrete actions are replaced by symbols or visualizations. The monasteries were the principal sites for the "clerical orientation" and historically sustained such sterilized versions of tantra. Most of the Euro-American scholars of chöd followed this route, in part, I believe, because as they read the history and lineage of Padampa and Machig, the texts they studied clearly point to the *Perfection of Insight* as a philosophical underpinning, and maybe also, in part, because of their own philosophical slant, reinforced by their clerical informants.

On the other hand, Edou might be willing to subsume chöd under some of the aspects of "shamanic orientation," or certainly the "ngakpa orientation," since he recognizes that its practitioners followed "the example of the early revealers, Dampa Sangyé and Machig, who preferred the (often outrageous) lay lifestyle of wandering yogis [i.e., ngakpa] to that of monastic community."[69] Edou acknowledges the unconventional lifestyle of the chöpa, but wants to preserve in them the "cultured" persona of someone following an Indian Buddhist doctrine. Some who take this line observe that chöd is also practiced in Nyingma monasteries.[70] However, in the Bön tradition, chöd is rarely practiced in the monastery. When it is practiced in the monastery, it is not by those in the dialectic school, but instead by those following the meditation curriculum, as we will see in more detail below. Also, in such cases it is usually practiced outside. Furthermore, as Yongdzin Tenzin Namdak asserts—at least from the Bön tradition's perspective—these monastic practices are to prepare the student so he can go to fearful places and actually perform chöd there.[71]

Edou may be objectifying the chöpas' experiences and trying to make them acceptable to a more "cultured" audience. This would fit the pattern that Mumford, drawing on Bakhtin, describes as the second stage in the dialogical process, where the ancient matrix (i.e., the shamanic/ngakpa aspects) is rejected in order to embrace the new directional identity, in this case Buddhism from India. In other words, Edou would not accept Samuel's contention that "certain aspects of Vajrāyana (Tantric) Buddhism as practiced in Tibet may be described as shamanic, in that they are centered around communication with an alternative mode of reality (that of the Tantric deities) via the alternate states of consciousness of Tantric yoga."[72]

I believe that it is crucial to recognize the similarities between the tantric techniques and the so-called shamanic trainings and to remember that the shamanic/ngakpa and the clerical orientations in Tibetan Buddhism share a common goal of enlightenment or the "bodhi" ideal (in Samuel's terminology).[73] Furthermore, it is also important to reiterate that the use of "shamanic" here has aspects of, but "is not restricted to the Siberian shamanic complex."[74] If we employ the concept of "shamanic orientation" and realize that it means that some clerical practitioners can still share some of its characteristics, in the same way that some lay practitioners can still share characteristics of the clerical orientation, it might help make the boundaries a little more flexible. Harding appears to go in this direction, pointing out that the chöpa's lifestyle "is conducive to the Buddhist ideal of non-attachment,"[75] thus finding some common ground between them.

Whatever stance we support, it is important to acknowledge the aspect of generosity involved in the practice of offering one's body (*lus sbyin*) that is embedded in the chöd practice. The practitioner employs his body, which is the "most powerful basis for all attachments and suffering, through the mind itself."[76] The body is the tool one uses to play the instruments (drum, bell, and thighbone) and dance and chant vigorously and, at the same time, it is the object of offering. As Norbu writes, "the human body is regarded as a precious vehicle for the attainment of realisation."[77] In this way, chöd should be seen as a vital practice that can lead to the final attainment of enlightenment, and thus I would agree with Edou and Harding in their underscoring its normative Buddhist orientation.

Although Edou seems to interpret chöd as a ritualized expression of Buddhist philosophy, he forewarns of any "reductionist interpretation"[78] which would undercut the purpose of the practice. For example, noted poet and novelist Brad Leithauser, writing about ghost stories (not chöd), claims that to approach them "purely as a battle with inner demons, however terrifying such may be, is to denature [them]."[79] Yet, since Edou utterly disconnects the chöd practice from any shamanic influence, his view could be considered as another form of reductionism. In contrast, Janet Gyatso and

Sarah Harding are more inclusive. Harding even says that some aspects of Chöd,

> whether from Indian sources or Machik's own syncretic system, obviously contain elements that can be identified with traditional shamanism. Given the adaptive nature of Buddhism, it would be surprising and disappointing if this were not the case.[80]

And Gyatso writes:

> We can find many elements of Gcod [chöd] that have similarities to what we know of shamanic beliefs and practices. . . . Nonetheless, the traditional positing of Indian Buddhism as the doctrinal, philosophical and textual source of Gcod cannot be dismissed as a mere attempt to embellish a shamanic rite with classical Buddhist trappings, for we find ample precedents for the theory and practice of Gcod throughout Buddhism. . . . The fact that shamanistic ideas and practices were assimilated by Buddhism itself at its earliest stages tempers any attempt to identify decisively the ultimate source of the Gcod technique.[81]

It is clear that there are many shamanic elements in tantra,[82] and these elements are certainly evident in the chöd practice, in particular in the "enacted dismemberment of the body in which 'parts' are identified with various demonic afflictions and powers of nature."[83] Harding also adds that another shamanic element "is that of contact with the spirit world and its connection to healing."[84] Mumford refers to chöd as "the most shamanic appearing of the lamas' rites."[85] Gyatso finds very interesting the similarity between "the early Tibetan image of the ascension of the *dmu* ladder and entrance through a 'sky-door' (*nam mkha' sgo 'byed*)"[86] and the ascension to upper purified realms through expelling one's consciousness in the transference practice (*'pho ba*), which also occurs in the chöd ritual. And Reynolds points out similarities between the chöd ritual and some of its shamanic antecedents, such as that of using the sound of a drum (which can induce trance), the singing and dancing, the blowing of a bone trumpet to summon the spirits, and the use of animal skins and other decorations.[87] Thus, using the "shamanic" within Tibetan traditions as an orientation that can include ngakpas, monks, and nuns (the latter two groups might be called "civilized shamans"), it is clear that shamanic rites can coexist with other views and practices such as the Mahāyāna viewpoint of the *Perfection of Insight* and tantric practices. As Harding observes: "It is virtually impossible to separate out what might have been preexisting elements and those of Buddhist origins, especially since all of it has been imbued with Buddhist intent."[88]

The Bön religion is distinctive for its accommodating approach to these "shamanic" aspects, which are incorporated in its own sūtric and tantric practices.[89] Therefore, examining chöd, the "most shamanic appearing of the lamas' rites," in the context of the Bön religion might provide a platform for arriving at a more integrated view. This integrated view corresponds to the third stage ("historical becoming") of Mumford's three dialogical stages that characterize the development of a tradition from an original matrix (stage one), to its rejection of, and resistance to, an alien culture (stage two), to a reconciliation and integration of both (stage three). In other words, at the third stage, the ancient matrix is reintegrated with the second stage of Buddhist directional identity, but now in a convivial way.

To contextualize chöd in the Bön tradition and go more deeply into the issue of shamanic orientation, even at the risk of opening a Pandora's box, I will next explore the understandings (and misunderstandings) that surround the relationship between Bön and Buddhism, especially as this relationship is understood in the extant scholarship. Perhaps this chöd ritual, despite being concerned with cutting through, may, ironically, help bridge some of these apparently opposing views.

Chöd in the Bön Religion

TIBETAN AND EURO-AMERICAN scholars have engaged in lengthy discussions about the origins of Bön. Bön sources claim their religion to be over eighteen thousand years old. Whatever the case may be, it is clear that it was well established in Tibet by the time Buddhism arrived there in the seventh century CE.[90] However, the prominence of Buddhism compared to Bön produced "religious polemical work quite hostile to Bon."[91] Dan Martin, who has studied this topic extensively, argues that "statements about the 'primitive animism of Bon' and its later 'transformation' or 'accommodation' (or 'plagiarism') have been repeated so often that they have achieved a status of cultural Truth."[92] Martin instead suggests:

> Bon as it existed during the last millennium represents an unusual, yet quite legitimate transmission of Buddhist teachings ultimately based on little-known Central Asian Buddhist traditions.[93]

The relationship between Bön and Chös, both being equivalents for the Sanskrit word *dharma* (that is, teachings about the true nature of phenomena and persons) for Bönpos and Buddhists respectively, is still controversial today. Some scholars, like Per Kvaerne, consider Bön to be a non-Buddhist religion. Their claim is based on "concepts of religious authority, legitimization and history"[94] that relate this tradition to its founder, Tonpa Shenrab Miwoche (*sTon pa gshen rab mi bo che*) instead of Buddha Shākyamuni. But others, such as Martin, Snellgrove, and Kvaerne (in an earlier publication)[95] describe Bön as a Buddhist sect—albeit an unorthodox one—based upon its practices and the doctrinal similarities of its "rituals, metaphysical doctrine and monastic discipline."[96] Bön and Buddhist teachings clearly share similar traits, and further historical research and perhaps new findings may be needed to clarify some of these issues. One problem is that Tibetan and Euro-American scholars have neglected to examine Bön texts, thereby silencing the Bön tradition by way of their *"docta ignorantia,"* which considers the Bön texts unworthy of their interest."[97] As D. Snellgrove and H. Richardson argue:

> The Bon-pos tend to become the scapegoat for everything that had rendered the Buddhist conversion of Tibet at all difficult, while most Tibetan Buddhists themselves remain almost innocently unaware of the great variety of pre-Buddhist beliefs and practices that they have absorbed as an accepted part of their daily thoughts and actions.[98]

However, some things have helped create a broader acceptance and understanding of the Bön tradition as a whole, for example, the Eastern Tibetan "nonsectarian" (*ris med*) movement of the nineteenth century and the present Dalai Lama's recognition of Bön as the fifth Tibetan School.[99]

Kvaerne states that the term "Bön" has the same range of connotations for its adherents (Bönpos) as "Chös" has for Buddhists.[100] This echoes an earlier conciliatory—and courageous—position taken by the Great Vairocana (*Be roi drag bag Chen mo*), a position presumably shared by a small group in eighth-century Tibet, who is said to have written: "Bön and Dharma differ only in terms of their disciples, their meaning is inseparable, a single essence."[101] Furthermore, Reynolds claims:

> For the Bonpos especially, the Dharma, whether it is called "chos" or "bon" in Tibetan, is not something sectarian, but it truly represents a Primordial Revelation, which is again and again revealed throughout time and history. It is not only primordial, but perennial. The Dharma is not simply the unique product of a particular historical period, namely, sixth century [BCE] North India.[102]

Interestingly, according to Snellgrove, "there is no word for 'Buddhism' in Tibetan."[103] Both the Bönpos and the Buddhists (followers of Chös) utilize the term "insider" (*nang pa*) for their followers, and "buddha" (*sangs rgyas*) to refer to the goal of enlightenment or being awakened. Germano explains:

> *Sangs rgyas* etymologically refers to how in this enlightenment experience the Buddha "clears away" (*sangs*) the sleep of igno-rance, and thus "unfolds" or "expands" (*rgyas*) the enlightened qualities (*yon tan*) of pristine awareness previously obscured by the clouds of ignorance enveloping it.[104]

In other words, Bön and Chös can be seen as different ways of expressing the teachings of a buddha.

Martin suggests that it is important to study the historical development of Bön without settling first the question of its origin:

> It may indeed be best to leave the question of origins to one side, and go on to try and learn as much as possible about the various aspects of this very old tradition as it existed in historical times until the present. If this brings no immediate conclusions about the questions of origins, it will certainly bring us a clearer picture of the entity whose origins we might wish to trace.[105]

Traditional Bön history claims that eighteen thousand years ago the Buddha Tonpa Shenrab Miwoche came to a region of central Asia known as Olmo Lungring (*'Ol mo lung ring*).[106] The teachings he gave there spread through-out all Central Asia, first to the regions of Tazig (*sTag gzig*) and Zhang Zhung (*Zhang zhung*), and then to Tibet, Kashmir, India, and China. G. Orofino reports that "according to Tibetan Bonpo tradition, the major part of its literature has been translated from the sacred language of Zhang zhung,"[107] with many Bönpo texts containing Zhang zhung words interspersed with Tibetan.[108] As Martin explains:

> The Bön traditions' own accounts of the history of their scrip-tures have them undergoing triple or even quadruple translations between the language of origin and the present Tibetan versions. The triply translated (*sum 'gyur*) texts generally went from Tazig to Zhang zhung to Tibetan, while the quadruply translated texts

generally went from 'divine language' (*lha'i skad*) to Sanskrit to Tazig to Zhang zhung to Tibetan.[109]

In these accounts, Tonpa Shenrab was Shākyamuni Buddha's teacher during two consecutive incarnations.[110] In the first of these, Tonpa Shenrab was named Chime Tsugphu (*'Chi med gtsug phud*, "Immortal Crowned One")[111] and Shākyamuni Buddha was one of his main disciples, Sangwa Dupa (*gsang ba 'dus pa*, "Essential Secret").[112] In the following life, in which Tonpa Shenrab was named Tonpa Shenrab, Shākyamuni Buddha was again one of his main disciples, Lhabu Dampa Karpo (*Lha'i bu dam pa dkar po*, "White Pure Son of the Gods").[113] Lhabu Dampa Karpo asked his teacher what he could do to help sentient beings, and Tonpa Shenrab told him that he should help the people in India who were following a wrong view. For that purpose, Tonpa Shenrab gave Lhabu Dampa Karpo an initiation so he would not forget the teachings in his future lives. Thus, in the next life he was born in India as Prince of the Shakya clan and taught, following the instructions previously given to him by his teacher, Tonpa Shenrab, thereby benefiting many sentient beings.[114]

Reynolds states, "it was principally in Zhangzhung [Zhang Zhung] and Tibet that the earlier version of Buddha's teachings called Bön have been preserved."[115] Both Reynolds and Martin mention the probable connection between the term "Bön" and Central Asia, in particular Tazig (today's Iran). Reynolds writes:

> Although some scholars [like Snellgrove] would derive the word *bon* from an old Tibetan verb '*bond-pa*', meaning to 'invoke the gods', corresponding to the Zhangzhungpa word *gyer*, it appears rather to come from the Tazigpa or Sogdian/Iranian word *bwn* meaning 'the Dharma'. This is another indication that the origin of Yungdrung Bön, or the Swastika Dharma, 'the Eternal Tradition', is to be found in the vast unknown spaces of Central Asia rather than historical Tibet.[116]

Martin, inspired by works of Christopher Beckwith, under whom he studied at Indiana University, suggests that "the Tibetan word *bon* might be a borrowing from Iranian Buddhists."[117] Martin himself does not support or reject this theory, but instead asserts that "it does fit nicely with the Bon claim that their religion originated in sTag gzig (Tazig)."[118] Heather Stoddard supports a possible connection between Iranian symbolism and Olmo Lungring,[119] but more research is needed to find clearer evidence. Therefore, until further research sheds more light on this topic, it is difficult to determine how much Bön and Chös encompass one another or to determine the extent and locus of this overlapping. Shardza, in his work on Bön history, *Treasury of Good Sayings*, writes:

> Enlightened Ones in their unceasing efforts and compassion as they labor for the welfare of sentient beings have made manifest temporary revelations of both *Bön* and *Chös*. We follow different doctrines to achieve different purposes.[120]

Klein and Wangyal gloss Shardza's quote stating that "'different purposes' arise through different doctrines being engaged, but their motivation and profundity are consonant."[121] This is in agreement with Reynold's earlier observation that the dharma is not simply the unique product of a particular historical period, but that it can take different forms according to the needs of the audience.

Traditional Bön accounts claim that Tonpa Shenrab's main teachings were the cycles of the Nine Ways or Nine Vehicles (*theg pa dgu*), and the Five Doors (*sgo lnga*).[122] The Nine Ways, especially from the Southern Treasure, were included in the monastic curriculum both in Tibet and in exile. This set of nine vehicles is unique and is distinct from similar divisions in the Nyingma tradition, and thus was the subject of the first Bön work to be translated into a Western language. The Nine Ways consists of four causal vehicles (*rgyu'i bon*, called "shamanic" by some Euro-American scholars) that include rituals, medicine, astrology, and divination; the subsequent result vehicles (*'bras bu'i bon*) of the sūtras and tantras; and the culminating Dzogchen (*rdzogs chen*, "Great Completeness").[123] Additionally, Yongdzin Tenzin Namdak states that because all nine vehicles were taught by Tonpa Shenrab, they are all considered legitimate paths to enlightenment.[124] In other words, whether "shamanic," sūtric, tantric or dzogchen, all have the bodhi ideal.

Bönpos themselves distinguish three kinds of Bön: (1) Bön (which retro-spectively is qualified as early or primitive), (2) Yungdrung (*g.yung drung*) or eternal Bön, and (3) new Bön (*bon gsar*). Early Bön is seen as an *ensemble* of popular religions, similar to what Stein calls "the nameless religion" or the "folk" tradition, as Tucci and others following him refer to it.[125] Yungdrung Bön is the religion that claims its origin in the teachings of Buddha Tonpa Shenrab and sees itself as a separate religion from Buddhism, even while acknowledging similarities. New Bön is a movement that surfaced in the sixteenth and seventeenth centuries from the interaction and amalgama-tion between Yungdrung Bön and Nyingma, the earliest Buddhist tradi-tion in Tibet.[126] Euro-American scholars usually doubt the veracity of the dating of the nine vehicles of Yungdrung Bön, usually dating them no ear-lier than the eighth or even tenth century.[127] Buddhists, even in the cases when they classify their teachings in nine vehicles, do not claim the causal vehicles as part of their teachings, much less as a separate vehicle.[128] In fact, even though Buddhists in Tibet have incorporated some of these prac-tices, they appear to have a protective feeling of exclusivity toward what in Yungdrung Bön are called the result vehicles.[129] Euro-American scholars, in particular Snellgrove, Martin, and Kvaerne, who accept the idea that Bön is an unorthodox form of Buddhism, believe that the Bön teachings come from the same source as Buddhism (namely, from Shākyamuni), but that they arrived in Tibet at different times and via different routes. Snellgrove believes that the teachings that were later called Bön were a form of Bud-dhism (mainly tantric) that began first in Zhang Zhung and then spread to Central Tibet. There, these teachings clashed with the Buddhist teach-ings that came directly from India.[130] It is clear that there was a Bön reli-gion in Tibet before the arrival of Buddhism around the seventh to eighth centuries CE, but it is hard to determine what teachings it comprised then. Today, Yungdrung Bön consists of all nine vehicles. As Kvaerne writes: "Bon was not a sinister perversion of Buddhism, but rather an eclectic tra-dition which, unlike Buddhism in Tibet, insisted on accentuating rather than denying its pre-Buddhist elements."[131] Therefore, I do not support the common misunderstanding that limits the Bön religion solely to the causal or "shamanic" vehicles, or the equally problematic identification of all Bön practitioners with the "result vehicles."[132]

THE BÖN TRADITION OF CHÖD

As many authors have noticed, Bön has its own chöd tradition, and it classifies its various texts in accordance with Gyatso's previous description:

> Bonpo tradition divides Gcod [chöd] practices in three types: a)
> *Zhi ba'i gcod* [peaceful chöd], e.g. the *A dkar zhi gcod*; b) *rGyas
> pa'i gcod* [extending chöd], e.g. the *Drung mu gcod chen* (published this year by Tshultrim Tashi); c) *dBang gi gcod* [powerful
> chöd], e.g. *mKha' 'gro gsang gcod* (the tantras of which are published in the present volume). The "new" Bon (*Bon gsar*) [tradition] adds a fourth, the *Drag po'i gcod* [wrathful chöd].[133]

The "Peaceful Chöd of the White *A*" (*A dkar zhi gcod*) was received in a transmission from Khandro Karmo Chenchig (*mKhan 'gro dkar mo chen gcig*, "Great White Lady Skygoer") by Marton Gyalek (*Mar ston rgyal legs*) alias *sMan gong ba*, born in 1062 in Tsongnyan Mengkong (*mTsho snya sman gong ba*)—North of Shigatse—in the Tibetan area of Tsang (*gTsang*). He was the disciple of Gongdzo Chenpo (*dGongs mdzod chen po*), the great hermit who promulgated the Instructions on the *A* (*A khrid*) system.[134]

Following chronologically, the "Great Yungdrung Chöd" (*Drung mu gcod chen*) "represents precepts from [Tongyung Thuchen] (*Stong rgyung mthu chen*) to [Shense Lhaje] (*Gshen gsas lha rje*) alias [Gode Phagpa Yungdrung Yeshe] (*Go lde 'phags pa g.yung drung ye shes*) and [Nyo Nyima Sherab] (*Gnyos nyi ma shes rab*), who flourished before 1310 [b. 1215]."[135]

Continuing the historical sequence, the fourteenth-century "Chöd of the Secret Skygoers" (*mKha' 'gro gsang gcod*) has been one of the most popular chöd sādhanas among the Bönpos. It was reinvigorated in the early part of the twentieth century, when many lamas who imparted teachings about it attracted a strong group of followers, and it remains very popular to the present day.[136] The English preface to the *Chöd of the Secret Skygoers* explains:

> The *snyan brgyud* [oral transmission] was received by [Tulku Tronyan Gyaltsen] (*Sprul sku khro gnyan rgyal mtshan*, 14th century).
> According to the Bstan-rtsis [chronology] of Nyima Tenzin (*Nyi*

ma bstan 'dzin), the snyan-brgyud was received in 1386. The ritual
texts of this cycle have already appeared in lithographic edition
from Delhi in 1966 published by [Chugso Khanpo Yundrung
Gyaltsen] (*Phyug so mkhan po gyung drung rgyal mtshan*).[137]

Among the New Bön chöd texts, there are precepts rediscovered by
Nyagter Sangngag Lingpa (*Nyag gter gsang sngags gling pa*) alias Walchung
Terchen (*dBal chung gter chen*, b. 1864),[138] and by his consort Khandro
Dechen Wangmo (*mKha' 'gro bde chen dbang mo*, b. 1868), among others.

Chöd is found in other texts as well (see appendix 3), but in fact it is outside of the fourfold division that we find the oldest Bön source for the chöd
practice: the *Mother Tantra*'s "Taking the Fearful Place as a Path" (*Ma rgyud
nyen sa lam khyer*), which is included in the *Secret Mother Tantra Cycle (Ma
rgyud gsang skor)*, "first promulgated among humanity by the Royal Shen
Milu Samlek [*Mi lus bsams legs*]."[139] Furthermore, Shardza Rinpoche's twen-
tieth-century explanation of this chöd text asserts that the *Mother Tantra*
(see figure 2) is the source of all four of the different kinds of chöd.[140] Shardza
praises it as the most excellent chöd, coming from the truth dimension (Tib.
bon sku, Skt. *dharmakāya*), with the earliest commentary by Milu Samlek,
and then guarded by the skygoers who protect the teachings of the path (*bya
ra ma*)—in particular Tshog gyi Dagmo (*Tshog gyi bdag mo*, "Pure Lady of
Accumulation").[141]

Regarding chöd's philosophical aspect, Yongdzin Tenzin Namdak states
that in the Bön tradition, and particularly from the dzogchen point of view,
there is not much similarity between the homonyms *gcod*, meaning severing or cutting, and *spyod*, meaning practice. And that this tradition is not
so much based on the *Perfection of Insight* teachings—although the aspect
of generosity is certainly there—but is mostly concerned with cutting the
base of ignorance (*ma rig pa*), which is equated with the demon of self-
grasping (*bdag 'dzin*).[142] This is the ignorance which leads us to cyclic existence or saṃsāra, to birth, death, and so forth. It is the king of demons, and
it has four ministers:[143] the believer in self-existence, the thinker of suffering of birth, the thinker of suffering of sickness, and the thinker of suffering of old age and death. Reflections of these come as visible demons that
harm oneself and others. As long-time Western chöd practitioner Tsultrim
Allione states:

FIGURE 2. Thangka of the *Secret Mother Tantra*. The central deity (*Sanchog Gyalpo* in union with *Chema Wotso*) is flanked by its retinue in the four directions, and the skygoers of the six paths of meditation, each of a different color. Top left: the green skygoer of Means, Dekche Drolma (*'Degs byed sgrol ma*); top right: the blue skygoer of Dream, Gyuma Chenmo (*rGyu ma chen mo*); bottom far left: the red skygoer of Fear (chöd), Tshog gyi Dagmo (*Tshogs kyi bdag mo*); bottom left: the yellow skygoer of Projection, Tharpe Lamdren (*Thar pa'i lam 'dren*); bottom right: the white skygoer of Sleep, Salche Dodralma (*gSal byed gdos bral ma*); and bottom far right: the brown skygoer of Death, Bardo Kundul (*Bar do kun 'dul*). Note that in the lower far left is Tshog gyi Dagmo, the red skygoer of the chöd practice.

Demons are not bloodthirsty ghouls waiting for us in dark places; they are within us, the forces that we find inside ourselves, the core of which is ego-clinging. Demons are our obsessions and fears, feelings of insecurity, chronic illnesses, or common problems like depression, anxiety, and addiction.[144]

In other words, it is through ignorance that we are led into saṃsāra: the cycle of birth, sickness, aging, death, and rebirth, and all the other issues that stem from that. The understanding of this cyclic process depends on one's capacity, and the practice of chöd in the Bön tradition is considered to be a powerful method to liberate one from this cycle. This is also the case in the Buddhist Dzogchen tradition.[145] According to Bön Dzogchen, one's perception of demons depends on one's capacity, and therefore they can be perceived either as existing outside of oneself or as part of oneself. We find this also in Machig Labdrön's words:

A demon actually is anything which obstructs one's progress towards enlightenment. That's what is known as a demon. Therefore, loving friends and relatives can become demons insofar as they obstruct one's liberation. Especially, there is no greater demon than one's self-grasping. As long as one has not cut this self-grasping, then all the demons are standing around with their mouths wide open.[146]

Through the practice of chöd one can recognize those obstructions or demons and use them as a bridge to reconnect to one's own nature, cutting the veils of one's ego (the self-grasping demon). Hence, chöd is a method that utilizes generosity as a means to cut the root of ignorance, clearing away all obstacles toward the understanding of one's true nature. In this practice one uses fear, pride, and even one's obsessions, feelings of insecurity, and so forth, realizing that it is only by cutting the self-grasper that one can understand the empty nature wisdom and go back to the source, the base, one's innate, primordial, and natural state.[147]

In short, we can say that the contemplative practice of chöd—from the Bön and Buddhist Dzogchen traditions—can be understood in various ways that go beyond (and include) "cutting through the attachment to one's body and ego" and "cutting through fear." They seem to involve a fusion of Tibetan and pre-Tibetan traditions with both an Indo-Tibetan and a Zhang Zhung–Tibetan Mahāyāna sūtra ethical framework, as well as with Tibetan tantra and dzogchen.

In the Buddhist tradition, the practice of chöd is traced back to the *Perfection of Insight Sūtra*, and later to the tantras,[148] but in the Bön tradition, it is traced back to the mother tantras.

THE MOTHER TANTRAS

The mother tantras "represent an important esoteric tradition of Bön belonging to the system of *A dkar ba* [the way of the white A], the seventh in the [stages of] Nine Ways of Bön (*theg pa rim dgu*)."[149] Among the Bön tantras the mother and the father tantras (*pha rgyud*) compose the highest classes.[150] Their method of practice is transformation (*bsgyur ba*), and whereas in the father tantras, the generation stage (*bskyed rim*) is emphasized (including intricate visualizations of deities and their maṇḍalas), in the mother tantras, the completion stage (*rdzogs rim*), where those visualizations are dissolved back into emptiness, is heightened.[151]

There are three cycles of mother tantras: outer, inner, and secret. For each, there is a root text or texts with a body of exegetical and liturgical works subordinate to the root text.[152] Milu Samlek wrote separate commentaries for each of the three cycles, but here I will focus on the secret cycle (*gsang skor*). The outer cycle (*phyi skor*) and inner cycle (*nang skor*), named "Sky Mandala of the Very Pure Lotus" (*rNam dag padma klong gi dkyil 'khor*) and "Cycle of the Great All-Clearing Loving Mother" (*Kun gsal byams ma chen mo'i rgyud*) respectively, were discovered at different times by different people. For example the *Inner Mother Tantra* texts were excavated earlier—Namkhai Norbu places it in 956 CE— by the Terton Trotsang Druglha (*Khro tshang brug lha*).[153] Martin reports that "three generations after their rediscovery, the *Loving Mother* [*Inner Mother Tantra*] texts were given to gZhon nu and were then passed along the same lineage with the Secret Mother Tantra literature."[154] Also Martin believes that Guru Nontse, who was the rediscoverer of the *Secret Mother Tantra*, "may be identified as an incarnation of one of the members of the earlier lineage."[155] The lineage is not just the mere historical transmission of the oral tradition, but is also the "transference of the 'charisma' (*byin brlabs*) [or blessings] of the institutor of the lineage."[156] Guru Nontse "was known in the Buddhist histories as Aya Bonpo Lhabun (*A ya bon po lha 'bum*), for he discovered many Nyingma Termas as well as Bonpo ones."[157]

The authorship of the *Secret Mother Tantra* is attributed "within the [root] texts themselves to Kuntu Zangpo (*Kun tu bzang po* [*Samantabhadra*, "Totally Good One"]), the Primordial Buddha Himself,"[158] a characteristic that is shared with other Bön and Nyingma high tantra and dzogchen texts. The *Mother Tantra* has the quite unique feature that the male aspect represents emptiness and the female aspect represents the clarity of the natural state, which is the reverse of what is found in other tantric texts. Furthermore, "the *Mother Tantra* is also unique among the Higher Tantras as a whole because, whereas it does employ the transformational process of the Kyerim [*bskeyd rim*, "generation stage"] and the Dzogrim [*rdzogs rim*, "completion stage"], its overall view is that of Dzogchen."[159] Dzogchen is the highest teaching in this tradition, and its method of practice is of self-liberation (*rang grol*) into the "non-dual single essence" or "unbounded wholeness" (*thig le nyag gcig*).[160]

According to the Bön tradition, the root texts of the *Secret Mother Tantra* are said to have originated in the dimension of Bön (Tib. *bon sku*, Skt. *dharmakāya*), where the male and female buddhas shared its teachings in the "eternal divine language" (*gyung drung lha'i skad*). The *Secret Mother Tantra* was then transmitted in Sanskrit to a retinue of skygoers, among whom the principal one was Zangza Ringtsun (*bZang za ring btsun*, "Goodwife Longexcellence"), an emanation of the great Cham Ma (*Byams ma*, "Loving Mother"):

> The Teachings of the *Mother Tantra* were revealed by her to three teachers who propagated the *Mother Tantra* in three different realms (*bsgrags pa skor gsum*): Yongsu Dagpa (*Yongs su dag pa*) among the [33] Devas in heaven, Yeshe Nyingpo (*Ye shes snying po*) among the Nagas in the netherworld, and Milu Samlek (*Mi lus bsam legs*) among humanity on earth.[161]

According to the *Secret Mother Tantra* texts, Milu Samlek then composed three commentaries in order to elucidate their meaning and transmitted the teachings to his disciple Mushen Namkha Nangwa Dogchen (*dMu gshen nam mkha' snang ba'i mdog can*). The latter, after practicing on the slopes of Mount Kailash, bestowed the initiation and instructions to the Bön pandit Anu Tragtak (*A nu 'phrag thag*), who in turn handed these teachings down to Sene Gau (*Sad na ga'u*) of Zhang Zhung. Sene Gau translated the teachings from Zhang zhung to Tibetan.[162] It was during Sene Gau's time that the first persecution of Bön teachings and practitioners took place, under the reign of the Tibetan Buddhist king Drigum Tsenpo (*Gri gum btsan po*, ca. 683 BCE), and therefore, "the custodianship of these texts of the *ma rgyud* was delivered by Sad ne ga'u into the hands of the six Dakinis of the Path, the Jarama (*bya ra ma*) or watchers,"[163] "who served as the 'treasure protectors.'"[164] Under king Trisong Detsen (*Khri srong lde btsan*, 790–848 CE), the Bönpos suffered a second persecution, and it was not until the twelfth century that the secret revelation of the mother tantras was rediscovered by Guru Nontse (*Gu ru rnon rtse*) in the rock of Dungpor (*Dung phor bkra shis*), near the village of Tanag (*rTa nag*) in the central province of Tsang, "hence this collection of Terma became known by the name of the *Dung phor ma*."[165] Guru Nontse then gave this collection of teachings to Zhonu (*gZhon nu*).

The *Secret Mother Tantra* text, like many of such discoveries, was discovered by "accident."[166] Guru Nontse, who was a hunter and a potter,[167] had hunted an antelope in the mountain and was chopping its bones on a rock when suddenly the rock broke apart. To his amazement, inside the rock he found a white silk cloth written on both sides and wrapped on a stick. The story goes that Zhonu, who was from Kham (East Tibet), had a dream in which the skygoers prophesied that he was to receive an important text. Sometime later, Guru Nontse in fact handed the *Secret Mother Tantra* silk cloth directly to him. Guru Nontse told Zhonu "since you have transferred from a divine status, your thoughts are pure and you are very quiet and relaxed. So copy the texts without anyone seeing them."[168] Then Zhonu went to Kham and copied the texts, but some time later Guru Nontse appeared unexpectedly and asked for the silk cloth, alleging that the skygoers wanted the cloth to be returned. Asking Zhonu whether he had seen the five loose, open-mouthed tigresses pass by at Dung phor,[169] Guru Nontse took the roll back.

According to Martin, Zhonu had copied all the *Secret Mother Tantra* texts, the three root texts (of base, path, and fruit), and the three commentaries on them by Milu Samlek (the short and medium commentaries were on one side of the roll, and the detailed commentary on the other side), but then could not find the most detailed commentary. But according to Yongdzin Tenzin Namdak and Reynolds (who was probably also informed by Tenzin Namdak), Guru Nontse appeared before Zhonu could finish copying the whole roll, so that Zhonu never got to the side of the longer commentary nor had time to copy down the short commentary. Thus, Yongdzin Tenzin Namdak states that Zhonu was able to copy only the medium-length commentary.[170]

All versions of the story agree that the silk roll which Guru Nontse gave to Zhonu contained the three root tantras together with the three sets of commentaries: the *Meaning Commentary: Solar Essence* (*don 'grel nyi ma'i snying po*), which is the abridged commentary;[171] the *Meditation Commentary: Mandala of the Sun* (*sgom 'grel nyi ma'i dkyil 'khor*), which is the intermediate-length commentary; and the *Explanation Commentary: Solar Rays* (*bshad 'grel nyi ma'i 'od zer*), which is the extended commentary, containing a word-by-word explanation of the three root texts of the *Secret Mother Tantra*. Martin agrees with Karmay in thinking that even when it is stated that Milu Samlek composed all three commentaries:

> It is not very clear which one we are dealing with. The commentary in hand [the *Secret Mother Tantra: Root Commentary of the Three Buddhahood Tantras* (*ma rgyud sangs rgyas rgyud gsum rtsa 'grel*)] states at the beginning (p. 207) that it is the *Meditation Commentary: The Solar Essence*, but on p. 208 it indicates that it is the *Meditation Commentary: The Mandala of the Sun*.[172]

As Martin points out, "there is some confusion in the titling of the texts" since *Solar Essence* is supposed to be the abridged or *Meaning Commentary* and not the *Meditation Commentary*.[173] Yongdzin Tenzin Namdak and John Reynolds do not view this as a problem. The discrepancy might arise from what it is believed Zhonu was able to copy down before hearing that the "five Dakinis riding on tigers had just appeared uttering dire prophesies."[174]

According to Yongdzin Tenzin Namdak, Zhonu was able to copy down the three root texts and only the intermediate-length commentary. Then Guru Nontse asked Zhonu to return the silk roll to him no matter how little had been copied since he had to return it. The silk cloth was never found again. Consequently, the *Meditation Commentary: Mandala of the Sun* is the only extant commentary.

Karmay's and Martin's confusion may derive from the inclusion of the enumeration of the forty-five wisdom spheres (*ye shes thig le zhe lnga*)—which is basically all of the abridged commentary—in the introduction of the extant text. There is no doubt that it is the *Meditation Commentary*; whether it is called *Solar Essence* or *Mandala of the Sun*, it is the *Meditation Commentary* in either case. I can think of two possible answers to this dilemma and propose them only as speculations. Limiting myself to the 1971 edition that Martin and Karmay were mainly working from, it is possible that giving the introduction the same name as the abridged commentary was a way of acknowledging that the medium-length commentary included the abridged one. But working from a later edition, which is not included in Karmay's catalogue since it is from 1985,[175] that same chapter 4 (or *nga* in the 1971 edition)—the first three chapters being the root texts—is actually called *Meditation Commentary: Mandala of the Sun*, which would then seem to resolve the conflict.[176] Martin acknowledges this and says that "most likely M [which is how he terms the 1971 edition] is mistaken, and the correct title of the set of commentaries available to us should be *Solar Mandala* [or *Mandala of the Sun*]."[177] The biggest difference seems to be in what is comprised under the other part of the title, namely, *Meditation Commentary*. Martin seems to follow Karmay in considering that it not only includes chapter *nga*, where the title is presented, but in fact contains all the commentary on the tantra of the base (chapters *nga* to *na*). I think this is only partially true. Karmay states that there is "no title" for the commentary on the path (chapters *pa* to *'a*), and Martin seems to agree with him.[178] I believe that in fact the same title extends all the way from chapters *nga* to *'a* and that the *Meditation Commentary: Mandala of the Sun* is the medium-length commentary on base, path, and fruit (even though Milu Samlek's commentary on the fruit is no longer extant) and not just on the base.[179]

Yongdzin Tenzin Namdak also believes that when Guru Nontse appeared to Zhonu in Kham, and the latter said he wanted to first finish copying the material, Guru Nontse told him, not only that the five tiger-like skygoers had come asking for it, but also that copying the long commentary was of no use because, in Tibet, there were no suitable students to receive this teaching. Guru Nontse said that Tibetan people had a deluded base, misunderstood the path, and therefore the fruit would be spoiled.[180] As far as Zhonu himself, Guru Nontse told him to practice what he had already copied and keep it for himself since other people would not understand it properly. The original copy was then returned.[181]

Historical and Traditional Understandings of the Authorship of the Secret Mother Tantra

Authorship of the *Secret Mother Tantra* is traditionally attributed to Milu Samlek, who is thought to have been king of Zhang Zhung and whose historicity is not questioned in the traditional accounts. Regardless of how one understands the concept of a text coming from the truth dimension through figures like Kuntu Zangpo, skygoers, and deities, this text had to emerge, at some point, from a historical individual. Therefore, bracketing how the act of composition is to be understood, it is important to determine the date the text emerged in history. This becomes all the more important here because the rediscovery date of the text that appears to contain the oldest version of chöd in the Bön tradition might be later than the composition date of another Bönpo chöd text. In other words, if the *Secret Mother Tantra* was composed in the time of its rediscoverer, Guru Nontse, and if we agree with the chronology that dates his birth in 1136 CE, then the *Peaceful Chöd of the White A* (*A dkar zhi gcod*)—composed around the late eleventh century—would be the older chöd text in the Bön tradition.

However, perhaps turning to what is known about the composer of the commentaries on the *Secret Mother Tantra* will provide some assistance in understanding when the root text was composed. Milu Samlek means "Human Body Good Thought." Martin, who explores the historicity of the figure of Human Body Good Thought, believes that he was a historical figure, although the stories about him are mythic:

> After giving the problem much thought, I have decided that the story of Human Body may be considered "legendary," but I must add immediately that I believe it partakes of history (as a legend, of course, it has its own history, and every legend, by definition, takes place in an aura of historicity).[182]

Martin paraphrases Vico, saying that every myth "must have once had a publically acknowledged ground of truth,"[183] and acknowledges that Milu Samlek was, as his name indicates, a human being. According to Bön traditional accounts, Milu Samlek lived "in the very remote past in a now vague geographical setting."[184] Thus, the dates of the commentaries attributed to him remain uncertain. Since Milu Samlek wrote commentaries for all three mother tantras—external, inner, and secret—his life is mentioned in all of them. Within the *Inner Mother Tantras* there is a text that focuses on Milu Samlek's life and the "problem of securing the family line."[185] Martin sees Milu Samlek's story as "a prototype for future generations to follow,"[186] the story of a king governing his kingdom as a spiritual realm, a maṇḍala. It is "a myth of an ideal king and his ideally constructed kingdom . . . a model capable of application in many different contexts—physical, psychological and spiritual as well as social."[187] Martin suggests that "Human Body's role in revealing the *Mother Tantras* is his most important definition. His story serves as a significant legitimating factor for later adherents of the tradition."[188] Those who believe that Milu Samlek was a human being believe that he thus was a historical figure, although some of the stories about him may be mythical.

In cataloguing this work, Samten Karmay ascribes most of the commentary on the *Secret Mother Tantra* to Milu Samlek and divides the text into four parts:[189]

1. chapters *ka* to *ga*, the three root texts, to which he ascribes no author;
2. chapters *nga* to *na*, a commentary on the *Root Text of the Base* (chapter *ka*), which Karmay attributes to Milu Samlek;
3. chapters *pa* to *'a*, a commentary on the *Root Text of the Path*—although it lacks the commentary on chapter eight, which contains the teachings on the expedient use of death (*'chi ba lam khyer*)—which Karmay also attributes to Milu Samlek; and
4. chapter *ya*, entitled *mKhan chen nyi ma rgyal mtshan gyi gsang mchog gi dbang lung thob tshul*, being "an account of a dream of the author,"[190] Mushen Nyima Gyaltsen (*dMu gshen nyi ma rgyal mtshan*, b. 1360).

Karmay believes Guru Nontse to be the rediscoverer of the first three parts, while the fourth part is Mushen Nyima Gyaltsen's own composition, the title of which could be translated as *The Mode of Achieving the Empowerment and*

Transmission of the Supreme Secret by the Great Teacher Nyima Gyaltsen.[191]
This work describes the transmission of the *Secret Mother Tantra* through
the lineage-holders. It is interesting to note as well, that in the 1985 edition
of the *Secret Mother Tantra* text, Mushen Nyima Gyaltsen's fourteenth-century composition is not included. Karmay attests that "this [added] work
belongs to the Collected Works of the author [Mushen Nyima Gyaltsen],"[192]
which could explain why Tshultrim Tashi, the editor of the 1985 edition, did
not include it in his edition.

So, it is certain that the Bön *Secret Mother Tantra* commentary, together
with its root texts, was rediscovered, centuries later, by Guru Nontse. After
a thorough analysis of the text, and particularly of the colophons (together
with Shardza's comments), Martin believes that the historical preface (chapter *nga*)—which is what he refers to as the *Meditation Commentary*— "was
written by the monk gZhon nu,[193] a direct disciple of the excavator of the
basic *Secret Mother Tantras* Gu ru rnon rtse, thus placing its composition in
the 12th century."[194] He is also open to other possibilities, stating that there
is "still nothing to definitely demonstrate his [Zhonu's] authorship of the
entire work"[195] (for example, chapter *nga*).[196]

Martin appears convinced that chapter *nga* was an "added preface," and
therefore "unlike many of the subsequent works, not ascribed to Human
Body Good Thought."[197] He believes that this preface was either composed
by Zhonu, or at least that "it is necessarily the work of a Tibetan from the
twelfth century or later."[198] Among the commentaries that Martin ascribes
to Milu Samlek, the *Commentary of the Path* (chapters *pa* to *'a*), which comprises the chöd practice (chapter *tsha*), is definitively included.[199]

As for the main issue of this section, the question of the historical origins
of the *Secret Mother Tantra*, there is data indicating that the chöd within the
Secret Mother Tantra is earlier than the *Peaceful Chöd of the White A* and
therefore, the oldest chöd within the Bön tradition:

(a) Accepting Guru Nontse to be *"before* the first *rab 'byung* [cycle][200] (beginning in 1027 A.D.)"[201]—instead of placing his birth in 1136 CE—would
place the activity of the *Secret Mother Tantra* excavator before the birth
of Marton Gyalek, the receiver of the transmission of the *Peaceful Chöd
of the White A.*[202]

(b) The absence of part of the *Commentary on the Path* and of all the *Com-*

mentary on the Fruit—but particularly the former— suggests that they existed earlier but were then lost. This is more likely than that the discoverer-author decided to skip commenting on some of the teachings that appear in the root texts.[203]

(c) If Milu Samlek is a historical figure, even without being able to pinpoint his precise historical setting, it is conceivable that he might have been alive before the tenth century. His life is mentioned in the *Inner Mother Tantra* text, which was rediscovered in 956 CE. And it seems clear from Martin's argument above that only chapter *nga* was added later—around the twelfth century— the rest (including the chapter on chöd) must have existed before that. According to Milu Samlek's story, that was in a very remote past (i.e., many centuries).[204]

(d) No historical individual is claimed to be the author of the root texts (including that of chöd). Because of point (b), the commentary for the chöd practice and the commentaries on the other chapters must have been written after the root texts, and because of point (c), the root texts must have been written before 956 CE. Thus the root texts of the *Secret Mother Tantra* must have been written at least a century prior to the *Peaceful Chöd of the White A*.

This argument supports the above proposal that the chöd within the *Secret Mother Tantra* is the oldest Bön version of this practice, providing potential historical evidence to support the traditional argument that the *Secret Mother Tantra*'s chöd is the source from which all the others stem. This view persists in today's traditional Bön accounts, as seen in Shardza Rinpoche's earlier assertion, to which Yongdzin Tenzin Namdak also subscribes. Under the limitations imposed by historical distance and the lack of more historically oriented material, I feel that there is enough historical (as well as traditional and anecdotal) evidence to conclude that the *Secret Mother Tantra* contains the oldest Bön version of the chöd practice.

THE STRUCTURE OF THE SECRET MOTHER TANTRA

The secret cycle of the *Mother Tantra* is known both as *Mother Tantra: The Tantric Cycle of the Sun of Compassion* (*Ma rgyud thugs rje nyi ma'i rgyud skor*) and *The Three Root Buddhahood Tantras with Commentaries*.[205] Interestingly enough, the 1985 edition uses the former title, whereas the 1971 edition uses the latter (*Ma rgyud sangs rgyas rgyud gsum rtsa 'grel*). Although both editions are almost identical in content, I will use the later one since it seems to be a more careful edition and thus more reliable.[206]

The text of the *Sun of Compassion* is divided in two ways: in the first, it is divided into forty-five wisdom spheres or *thigles* (*thig le*), which the introduction enumerates, and in the second, into eighteen chapters, six for each of the three buddhahood tantras of base, path, and fruit. The chöd practice is found in the second tantra (i.e., the path) and is the twenty-second wisdom sphere: the *Sphere of Accumulation, the Completion/Perfection of the Accomplishment of Wisdom* (*Tshogs kyi thig le ye shes grub la rdzogs*). An overview of the outline for all three tantras will be helpful in order to understand the structure of the *Secret Mother Tantra* cycle as a whole and the place of chöd in it.[207]

When divided in the more traditional way, the *Secret Mother Tantra* is first divided into three parts: base (*gzhi*), path (*lam*), and fruit (*'bras*), which are subdivided into six parts each, making altogether eighteen steps that the practitioner should pursue in order to attain liberation. In the 1985 edition, the first three chapters are the three root tantras, and chapter four (*nga*), as was discussed earlier, is what Martin calls the historical preface. Then, the text is divided as follows:

I. The commentary on the six facets of the base
    1. "The total-base of the spontaneously manifested wisdom teachings" (*kun gzhi ye shes lhun grub bstan pa*), which is an explanation of the introduction to the natural state (chapter 5)
    2. "The appearing-base of the spontaneously manifested three buddha-dimensions" (*snang gzhi sku gsum lhun grub*): a) truth buddha-dimension (Tib. *bon sku*, Skt. *dharmakāya*), b) completed buddha-dimension (Tib. *rdzogs sku*, Skt. *saṃbhogakāya*), and c) manifested buddha-dimension (Tib. *sprul sku*, Skt. *nirmāṇakāya*) (chapter 6)[208]
    3. "The empty-base of the spontaneously manifested four buddha-dimensions" (*stong gzhi sku bzhi lhun grub*), where the four buddha-dimensions are explained in four different chapters in terms of channels (Tib. *rtsa*, Skt. *nāḍī*), vital breath (Tib. *rlung*, Skt. *prāṇa*), essential sphere (Tib. *thig le*, Skt. *bindu*), and behavior (Tib. *spyod*

pa, Skt. *bhoga* or *caryā*), each explained in a different chapter (chapters 7 to 10 respectively)

4. "The scriptural-base of the spontaneously manifested four empowerments" (*lung gzhi dbang bzhi lhun grub*): a) external (*phyi ba*), b) internal (*nang ba*), c) secret (*gsang ba*), and d) esoteric or ultrasecret (*yang gsang ba*) (chapter 11)

5. "The meaning-base of the spontaneously manifested view and behavior" (*don gzhi lta spyod lhun grub*), where instructions for familiarizing oneself with methods for stabilization practice (*zhi gnas*) are given (chapter 12)

6. "The activity-base of the spontaneously manifested action" (*las gzhi 'phrin las lhun grub*) (chapter 13)

Chapter 14 relates the history of the lineage.

II. The six parts of the path
   1. The path of accumulation (*tshogs lam*) (chapter 15)
   2. The path of union (*sByor lam*) (chapter 16)
   3. The path of seeing (*thong lam*) (chapter 17)
   4. The path of meditation (sG*om lam*) (chapters 18 to 22)

   The path of meditation comprises six methods or "six principles of expediency" (*lam khyer drug*): [209]

   - The expedient use of means, devoted mainly to the channels and vital breath, which corresponds to "the sphere of the elements" (*byung ba'i thig le*) (chapter 18)
   - The expedient use of dream (*rmi lam*), which corresponds to "the sphere of selfhood" (*bDag nyid thig le*) (chapter 19)
   - The expedient use of fear, which is the practice of chöd or the practice of fearful places (*gnyan sa lam*), which corresponds to "the sphere of accumulation" (*tshogs gyi thig le*) (chapter 20)
   - The expedient use of projection (*'pho ba*), which corresponds to "the sphere of accomplishing" (*grub pa'i thig le*) (chapter 21)
   - The expedient use of death, which explains the after-death intermediate states (*bar do*) and corresponds to "the sphere of abiding" (*gNas gyi thig le*). Its commentary has been missing since its rediscovery by Guru Nontse.

- The expedient use of sleep (*gnyid pa lam khyer*), which corresponds to "the sphere of clarity" (*gSal ba'i thig le*) (chapter 22)
5. The path of freedom (*thar lam*) (chapter 23)
6. The path of ripening and liberation (*sMin grol lam*) (chapters 24 and 25)[210]

III. The six parts of the fruit[211]
   1. The fruit of excellence (*mChog 'bras*)
   2. The fruit of meaning (*don 'bras*)
   3. The fruit of [practice] session (*thun 'bras*)
   4. The fruit of nature (*ngang 'bras*)
   5. The fruit of space (*kLong 'bras*)
   6. The fruit of nonexistence (*med 'bras*)

The eighteen parts together are the deep teachings of exalted liberation (*rnam grol*). As seen above, chöd is the third practice among the six principles of expediency: the expedient use of fear. When divided into forty-five wisdom spheres, chöd is the twenty-second, the sphere of accumulation, where wisdom is perfected in accomplishment or realization (*thig le ye shes grub la rdzogs*).[212] The inclusion of chöd within the six methods seems to be unique to the Bön system. As mentioned earlier, chöd is also found in an abbreviated form in the main practice of the *Secret Mother Tantra*, the *Threefold Practice of the Authentic Wisdom*[213] (*dGongs spyod rnam gsum*), which refers to the practice of the teacher (*bla ma*), tutelary deity (*yi dam*), and skygoer (*mkha' 'gro*). In the third, the skygoer (as an aspect of oneself) comes out and chops up one's body, liberating the meditator "from the bonds of all grasping at reality," while the practitioner performs the chopping gesture (*phyag rgya, mudrā*).[214] This practice is found in the chapter of the path of freedom.

The base represents the view, the path the practice, and the fruit the result. The importance of the path lies in the explanation of which practices should be done and how to practice them. In particular, the path of meditation offers the six methods, corresponding to the six skygoers who guard the practices of the path, among which chöd is the third, and is represented by the red skygoer, the Lady of Accumulation (*Tshog gyi Dagmo*)—see figure 2 above.

THE CHÖD OF THE *SECRET MOTHER TANTRA*

As explained above, the chöd practice appears in the *Secret Mother Tantra* briefly as part of the *Threefold Practice*, and more extensively as the third among the six expedient means. The latter is called the *Commentary of the Fearful Place within the Sun of Compassion of the Mother Tantra* (*Ma rgyud thugs rje nyi ma'i gnyan sa lam du khyer ba'i 'grel pa*), which corresponds to chapter 20 (pages 655 to 681) of the 1985 edition. This chapter explains the chöd practice, but does not provide an actual practice liturgy. Therefore, I will provide an overview of the *Commentary of the Fearful Place* chapter[215] and include in appendix 1 a translation of what is probably the most popular chöd practice liturgy among Bönpos today: Shardza's *Laughter of the Skygoers* (see figure 3).

FIGURE 3. Thangka of Shardza Rinpoche. Painted by Kalsang Nyima.

The *Fearful Place* chapter starts with prostrations to Kuntu Zangpo, after which the six principles of expediency are explained as an approach to the path of tantra that enables the practitioner to traverse the second to the seventh bodhisattvic grounds (one practice per ground). These six essential teachings of the path of meditation are also equated with the mode of applying (*sbyar*) the six senses or powers (*dbang po*). These six powers are: life (*srog*), knowledge (*rtog*), cutting (*gcod*), understanding (*shes*), awareness (*rig pa*), and clarity (*gsal ba*), respectively. All these powers are potentially the pure aspects of a buddha's insight.

The one that concerns us here, the "power of cutting" (*gcod pa'i dbang po*), is related to direct perception (*mngon sum*) since it cuts through the delusion of ignorance.[216] Each of the five words that compose the title *Tshogs-kyi Thig-le Ye-shes Grub-la rDzogs* represent an internal section of this chapter.

Tshogs are the teachings of illusory accumulation, that is, learning the illusory nature of things, in order to properly accumulate merit. *Thig le* is the absolute integration with the single nature. *Ye shes* is the profound wisdom caused as a product of a frightening [place] (or establishing wisdom through fear). *Grub* is the accomplishment of cutting illnesses and energetic disturbances, and *rDzogs* is the explanation of the signs of completion or perfection.

This chöd text is comprehensive. Even though it does not include instructions on how to perform the practice—its "means of achievement" (*sgrub thabs, sādhana*)—it does provide the context for it and enough explanation to help one understand the chöd practice as a whole. What follows is an annotated table of contents (*sa bcad* or *dkar chag*), which I believe will provide the reader with a closer relationship to this text and its meaning.

I. The general meaning of *Tshogs* has three divisions: a) going to a frightening place, b) distribution of the great accumulation without desire, and c) directly teaching the illusory [nature of phenomena].

    a) Going to a frightening place

    b) Distribution of the great accumulation without desire

       1. Differentiating with wisdom

       2. Inviting the owner of accumulation

       3. Distributing the great accumulation to all

       4. Making the offerings without desire

c) Directly teaching/showing the illusory [nature of phenomena]

    1. Teachings of illusion proceeding from external to internal (i.e., from the eight different places of the eight classes of beings, and so forth)

    2. Teachings of illusion emanated from internal to external [Internal afflictions become visible as the disturbances of the eight classes of beings.]

    3. Realizing the root of illusion as anger or desire [Here it is important to comprehend illusion vis à vis the correct understanding of how things really are from the point of view of abiding in the natural state.]²¹⁷

II. The general meaning of *Thig le* has no divisions, illustrating its single nature or unbounded wholeness.

III. The general meaning of *Ye shes* has three divisions: a) the wisdom that establishes [oneself] in a frightening place or object, b) the wisdom that confronts the frightening object, and c) the wisdom that focuses (*the pa*) on a very frightening object, as in cornering it.

IV. The general meaning of *Grub* has three methods for cutting illnesses and energetic disturbances: a) to establish the frightening object with meditative concentration, b) to establish the frightening object with frightening behavior, and c) to practice earnestly the four: the triad of view, meditation, and conduct, and their result.

V. The general meaning of *rDzogs* has three divisions of the explanations of the signs of perfection: a) identifying the significant signs of accomplishment, b) protecting oneself in order not to relapse (i.e., that the disturbances will not return), and c) building on the important points and establishing them as nails so that the disturbances will never return.²¹⁸

As we can see from this brief description, the *Mother Tantra* chöd emphasizes the importance of abiding in the natural state and understanding the illusory nature of things and oneself. This is heightened by going to frightening places and performing various offerings to the beings there. The final offering is said to be that of offering one's own body, overcoming in this manner all kinds of fear, and becoming free from grasping. When one can offer oneself indiscriminately to all beings, without desire or expectations of any kind of reward, one learns the illusory nature of those beings and of oneself. This illusion is said to be based on the afflictions, rooted in ignorance or deluded awareness (*ma rig pa*), and its two main branches: desire (*'dod chags*) and anger (*zhe sdang*).

Chöd cuts the root of that illusion by eliminating the fear that attaches one to one's body after mistaking the body for oneself. By focusing on frightening objects, confronting them, cornering them, and being comfortable in or with them, fear leads to liberation from deluded awareness. It also brings, as a secondary benefit, the ability to repel physical and mental illnesses and energetic disturbances by meditating on what and who is being frightened by them. Being able to sustain that comprehension of the illusory nature of phenomena (including oneself) as one's view helps one recognize one's accomplishments in meditation, conduct, and result. This protects one from returning to the usual delusion and establishes instead a clear awareness (*rig pa*).

THE *SECRET MOTHER TANTRA* LINEAGE

The *Secret Mother Tantra* teachings, which contain the first chöd in the Bön tradition, are said to have originated in the truth dimension, where the original language was the eternal divine language shared by the primordial buddhas, male and female, Kuntu Zangpo and Kuntu Zangmo (Tib. *Kun tu bzang mo*, Skt. *samantabhadrī*, "Totally Good Lady"), and the skygoers. In the land of the thirty-three gods, on the summit of Mount Meru, the teachings were spoken in Sanskrit and handed down to the skygoer Zangza Ringtsun and her retinue, and then to Sangwa Dupa—of whom Buddha Shākyamuni is considered to be a reincarnation—who received them in the Bön Tazig language in the Shen country of Olmo Lung-ring.

Milu Samlek then received the teachings in the Zhang zhung Mar language (*zhang zhung smar gyi skad*) at Gyakhar Bachod (*rGya mkhar ba chod*).[219] Mushen Namkha Nangwa Dogchen, "the sage who possessed the color of the appearance of the sky," received the teachings from Milu Samlek and went to practice "on the slopes of Mount Meru."[220] Then Anu

Thragthak, the Bön pandit of Tazig, received the teachings, practiced the "three hundred and sixty great austerities,"[221] and then taught them in the language of the Tibetan kingdom, Pugyal Tibetan (*pu rgyal bod kyi skad*), to Sene Gau of Zhang Zhung, who in turn gave them to the skygoers of the path to protect.

A few centuries later, they were rediscovered by Guru Nontse, who handed them to Zhonu. The latter passed the teachings to the two meditators (*sGom pa*): Gompa Yungdrung Kyab (*sGom pa g.yung drung skyab*) and Gompa Rinchen Pal (*sGom pa rin chen dpal*). They taught Kadam Yeshe Gyaltsen (*bKa' gdams ye shes rgyal mtshan*), who in turn gave the teachings to both Zhangton Sonam Palden (*Zhang ston bsod nams dpal ldan*) and his nephew Zhangton Sonam Gyaltsen (*Zhang ston bsod nams rgyal mtshan*). Then, they transmitted them to Mushen Nyima Gyaltsen (*dMu gshen nyi ma rgyal mtshan*, b. 1360).[222]

From Mushen Nyima Gyaltsen until our time the lineage remains unbroken, reaching in the nineteenth and twentieth centuries Shardza Tashi Gyaltsen, Yongdzin Sangye Tenzin (Yongdzin Tenzin Namdak's teacher), and then Yongdzin Tenzin Namdak himself.[223] Reynolds acknowledges Yongdzin Tenzin Namdak's importance in this lineage, writing:

> Lopon [Yongdzin] Tenzin Namdak remains the leading exponent of the Mother Tantra system outside Tibet. Because of its complexity and profundity, the Mother Tantra was not studied or practiced as much as the Father Tantras [and so forth] in Bonpo monasteries.[224]

THE PRACTICE OF CHÖD AMONG BÖNPOS TODAY

Although, as explained earlier, the *Perfection of Insight Sūtra* is not the main source of the chöd practice in the Bön tradition, "offering" is an important part of the practice. Offering or generosity (*sbyin pa*) is the first among the six perfections, which culminate in the perfection of insight (*shes rab phar phyin*). And as Yongdzin Tenzin Namdak asserts, "if one lacks any of them, one cannot progress properly along that path."[225] Moreover, Śāntideva's "classic" on this subject, the *Bodhicaryāvatāra*, explains the importance of not limiting generosity to the first perfection. In chapter five, Śāntideva says:

The perfection of generosity is said to result from the mental attitude of relinquishing all that one has to all people, together with the fruit of that act. Therefore the perfection is the mental attitude itself.[226]

Generosity is the "mental attitude" that is the foundation of the altruistic intention. Generosity and insight are the two main ingredients in developing the mind of enlightenment (Tib. *byang chub sems*, Tib. *bodhicitta*) in the Mahāyāna vehicle. The Bön tradition has similar *Perfection of Insight* teachings to that of Buddhism, with the same six perfections (*phar phyin drug*) condensed from ten.[227] Furthermore, Bönpos claim that it was Tonpa Shenrab who originally taught the *Perfection of Insight* teachings.[228] Among the nine Bön vehicles of the southern treasure, the *Perfection of Insight Sūtra* is located in the sixth (*drag srong theg pa*), the "Way of the Great Ascetics."[229]

Reiko Ohnuma sees a parallel between the "gift of the body" tales of bodhisattvas and the *ātma-parityāga* ("self-sacrifice") stories of the Buddha and conceives of the latter as being about the gift of the body of dharma, the *dharmakāya*. She reaches the conclusion that "perhaps what these stories attempt to suggest is that the Buddha's gift of dharma to living beings should emotionally be experienced as equivalent to someone who slices up his own body and gives his flesh away."[230] This is the feeling of total generosity; the gift to which the chöpa can relate when doing his practice.[231] What is interesting about Ohnuma's study is that she sees the *jātaka* tales as being, not just about the generous and compassionate offering of the physical body, but also about the Buddha's offering of the enlightened-body dimension of the teachings.[232] The offering of the body of dharma (chös or bön) thus seems to be the ultimate offering. The experience of that kind of generosity may be similar to the experience of the dzogchen view in chöd, where one has given everything, including the teachings, and thus rests in the naked awareness of the natural state. Similarly, Kalu Rinpoche said:

If you feel like going to a cemetery, fine, but this is not necessary. A cemetery is a place where corpses and frightening and repulsive things are found. Milarepa said that we permanently have a corpse at our disposal, it is our body! There is even another cemetery, the greatest of all cemeteries, it is the place where all our thoughts and emotions come to die.[233]

This total self-sacrifice is what permits the connection with everything and everyone; nothing and no one is excluded.

In the chöd ritual, different terms have the meaning of "offering," such as "generosity/offering of the body" (*lus sbyin*), and "the sphere of offering or accumulation" (*tshogs gyi thig le*). The more common word for offering is *mchod* and is a homonym of *gcod*. Yongdzin Tenzin Namdak says that there is no relation between them; nevertheless, chöd (*gcod*) is considered to be one of the four general offerings (*mchod*)—together with the smoke offering (*sang mchod*), water offering (*chu/chab gtor*), and burnt food offering (*sur mchod*)—that Bönpos perform daily at Tritsan Norbutse Monastery (*Khri brtan nor bu rtse*).[234]

As a tantric practice of the mother tantras, chöd is included within the seventh—the "Way of Pure Sound [of the white A]"—of the nine vehicles of Bön's southern treasure, but the other three methods of offering belong to the causal vehicles.[235] Yongdzin Tenzin Namdak states that the methods of the first three offerings are found among the four causal vehicles, but really that varies according to the practitioner: "If a practitioner is a dzogchenpa, then his practice of those methods are dzogchen."[236] Of course, this applies to all methods of practice.

Because of its terrifying nature, chöd is not included among the monastic curriculum; but lay practitioners and monks who follow the meditation school curriculum (and not the dialectic school's) in Menri Monastery (*sMan ri*) in Dolanji, India and in Tritsan Norbutse in Kathmandu, Nepal, do practice chöd as the fourth offering.[237] Except for special occasions, only the monks following the meditation school perform the four offerings, which they include as part of their daily practice. In the early morning, around 4 a.m. (4:30 a.m. in the winter), the smoke offering ceremony is performed by one or two monks on behalf of the whole monastery. This is an offering of smoke or incense (usually including juniper branches and foliage) which has a powerful purificatory effect on the place, and it is directed specifically to the local protectors, the eight classes of beings, and the beings of the six realms. (Some monks might practice it individually in their own rooms, but usually with just a stick of incense.)

In the late morning, around 11 a.m., the meditation group includes the water offering as part of its meditation session. This offering is considered a very pure and simple one, directed to all four guests, in which clean, fresh water is poured on flower petals and grains that are arranged in nine bowls in a circular pattern, with one remaining in the center.[238] When performing this offering, it is common to request that the deities help sentient beings to satisfy their needs, or reorient those who are lost.

In the afternoon, around 4 p.m., the burnt food offering is included as part of the meditation session. This offering is directed primarily to the hungry ghosts and spirits of those who passed away, and it consists of burning all types of food that give off a good smell, primarily roasted barley flour (*rtsam pa*), butter, oil, medicine, and grains—the smell being the support which satisfies all their desires.[239]

The water offering and the burnt food offering are done at the very end of the meditation session. Usually these sessions begin with prayers (mostly from the *Threefold Practice of the Secret Mother Tantra*, which interestingly has a very brief offering of the body component),[240] followed by the central part of the practice, and concluding with prayers in which these offerings are included.

Finally, at night, around 9 p.m., chöd is performed as part of the session. As mentioned earlier, not only is it thought to be a very powerful means both to help all sentient beings through practicing generosity and to develop bodhicitta, but most importantly the ultimate benefit is to develop the nondual state of meditation. Therefore this session also begins with prayers, followed by stabilizing in the natural meditative state in which the chöd practice is begun, accompanied by the rhythm of the damaru and the Bönpo bell, shang (*gshang*) or silnyen (*ksil snyan*). Chöd is performed at night to increase its terrifying aspect. When it is practiced within the monastery complex, doing it at night prevents outsiders from being there, but also provokes fear similar to that evoked by a charnel ground or any of the other classical terrifying localities in which one is supposed to perform chöd.

When practiced in this way, the monks use the short sādhana created by Shardza Tashi Gyaltsen, *Laughter of the Skygoers*, in which they transform into the skgoer Kalzang Ma (see figures 4 and 5). The one in the *Secret Mother Tantra*, "Taking the Fearful Place as a Path," is a more elaborate and thorough chöd text, but does not contain a sādhana. As we can infer from

FIGURE 4. Thangka of Kalzang Ma.

the brief explanation of its index above, this text describes different aspects of chöd and elaborates concepts that explicate in depth the meaning of chöd. *Laughter of the Skygoers* is a text that comprises all aspects of the chöd practice, condensed in a liturgical form; the text consists of lyrics to be read aloud when performing the practice. This sādhana is very popular among Bönpos

FIGURE 5. Khandro Rinpoche, who is believed to be the incarnation of Kalzang Ma, sitting next to Tenzin Wangyal Rinpoche in Jeri Monastery, Tibet. Photo by the author.

today because it is a short but comprehensive sādhana and because it was composed by a recent master of the lineage, thus the connection is more direct and "warm."[241] During my field work I have found, both in the Bön communities in exile and when chöd is taught to Western practitioners, that the theory is derived from the *Mother Tantra*, mostly from "Taking the Fearful Place as a Path," and the liturgy is taught from Shardza's *Laughter of the Skygoers.*[242] Therefore, I have included a translation and explanation of Shardza's text in appendix 1.

Lay practitioners also perform this practice when on pilgrimage, and sometimes the ritual is performed in order to cure illnesses or remove obstacles. Donatella Rossi observes:

> Chöd practice and performance is requested and deemed truly effective as far as funerary issues, epidemics, psycho-physical illnesses and disturbances, and harmonizing the relations with the natural and elemental environment at large are concerned.[243]

The social role of chöd and especially its use as a healing practice is a very interesting topic, but unfortunately outside of the scope of the present study.[244] Nevertheless, the description of the implements the chöpa uses might provide some insight into this healing component and trigger one's curiosity about the kind of "ambiance" that it creates for those participating in or observing the fascinating performance of this practice.

IMPLEMENTS USED IN THE PRACTICE

The main implements used in the chöd practice of the Bön tradition are a drum or damaru, a thighbone trumpet or kangling (*rkang gling*), and a flat bell, a shang or a smaller silnyen.[245] The cover of this book shows a Bön chöpa holding a damaru in his right hand and a kangling in his left (the same hand with which he would use the bell—which, therefore, is not shown).[246] These implements however are not essential to the practice. The *Secret Mother Tantra* chöd, for example, does not mention them; but they may have been added later to help the practitioner connect with the spirits and create an "ambiance" that can facilitate overcoming of fear, understanding impermanence (particularly when using bone implements), and entering into the natural state.[247] These implements are musical instruments and since they are usually made of bone, they set the mood of a fearful place. The charnel ground setting is also similar to the way some tantric deities are depicted, for example, as stepping on corpses and wearing such bone ornaments as skull necklaces, waistband, and so forth. The music seems to wake up those beings and the fearful feelings in the practitioner, so he can then cut the fear that enhances the perception of duality.

The damaru (see figure 6) is traditionally made of two skulls (1) joined at their apices; one of a sixteen-year-old boy and one of a similarly aged girl (representing method and insight respectively). It is best if these young children had died in an accident, not through illness. The best skull is that which is in one piece and has no lines, the color of an eggshell, and a fontanel large enough so that when filled with yogurt it cannot hold it (this is a good sign of the person's having accomplished the transference or phowa practice).[248] Of course, finding such a skull is not an easy task, therefore skulls of lesser quality, that is, without these precise characteristics, are used. Indeed, today most are wooden damarus shaped to resemble skulls.[249]

The drum is constructed by stretching and gluing skins across the open ends of the hemispheres (2) and attaching two diametrically opposed strings

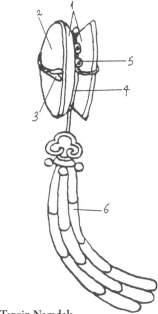

FIGURE 6. Damaru.
Illustration by Yongdzin Tenzin Namdak.

to the waist of the drum (4), from which are suspended pellet strikers (3). Also a garland of bells (*dril bu'i gyer kha*) is mounted to the drum (5) As a decoration, a colorful silk tail is usually attached to the bottom of the damaru (6).[250]

The skulls and their desired characteristics seem to be the most symbolic aspect of the damaru. They represent the state of union of method and insight, the nondual state of mind. Possibly the sign of the transference opening is important to help one expel the mind correctly when one transforms into the deity.

The shang or silnyen is made of a metal alloy[251] that can produce a beautiful sound as part of the offering (see figure 7). It is round, flat, and has three concentric circles representing the three wheels of teaching: sūtra, tantra, and dzogchen (1). Sometimes they are carved with the eight auspicious symbols. The metal represents the empty nature (2), and the wooden clapper represents clarity (3). The sound represents the union of clarity and emptiness. The precious jewels like dzi (*gzi*, Tibetan lucky stone), semiprecious stones, or corals that adorn the thread (4) which holds the clapper represent the spontaneous manifestation (*lhun grub*). The holder knot (an endless knot as one of the eight auspicious symbols) represents the pure teaching (5).[252] A silk tail decoration, similar to that of the damaru, may be attached under the holder knot as well (6).

FIGURE 7. Shang or silnyen.
Illustration by Katy Chamberlain.

The kangling is used to call the spirits and the best quality comes from the thighbone of a teenage child who died in an accident (see figure 8). If it is from a boy, it should be from his right leg, if from a girl, from her left leg. Dorje and Ellingson describe its construction as follows:

> The trumpet consists of a leg bone cut off about 30 cm. from the knee joint. Two holes cut in the ends of the projecting knobs (epiphyseal condyles) of the knee joint form the trumpet's double bell [(1)], while a conical recess cut into the other end of the piece of bone forms the mouthpiece [(2)].[253]

The top part of the thighbone represents the path of ghosts and evil spirits (3), while the part that becomes flat is the skygoers' dancing stage—where they push down the evil (4). On the side it should have a small hole signifying the yogi's insight (5). The double bell consists of two holes, of which

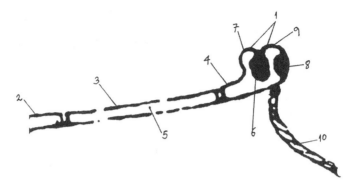

FIGURE 8. Kangling. Illustration by Yongdzin Tenzin Namdak.

the right one should be bigger so as to represent insight (6), thus creating a higher knob symbolizing the divinity (7). The left hole should be smaller, so as to represent the faults (8), and thus creating a lower knob signifying the demons (9). Again, kanglings with all these qualifications are very hard to find. But in contrast to the damaru, all kanglings are made of bone, although I have seen some made from animal bone instead of human.[254] Often they are decorated by encasing the mouthpiece and bell with silver (or other metals) and jewels, or wrapping them in leather or other skins. Sometimes the kangling is wrapped in metal or leather, partially or totally. A leather strip or skin can be added to the bottom of the double bell, which may be used as a whip to tame the ghost and demons (10).

According to Dorje and Ellingson, "each melody is an acoustic expression of the emotional character of its generating mantra."[255] In the *Laughter of the Skygoers*, it does seem to correspond to the emotional character of the calling, but not necessarily linked with a mantra. Whatever the case may be, it is unquestionable that there is a strong link between the chöd practice and the music performed during it.

Conclusion

THE MELODY is as enchanting as the chöd practice itself. Many Western practitioners are fascinated with the practice and its powerful melody, although not many scholars have written about it. Among Tibetans too, chöd remains more prominent in the realm of the ngakpas. My wonderful and colorful first teacher, Ngakpa Yeshe Dorje Rinpoche, sang this melody as he wandered through 108 scary places in Tibet, practicing chöd with the damaru, bell, and kangling. Once in India, and with the support of His Holiness the Dalai Lama—for whom he became his "weatherman," he established Zilnon Kagye Ling in Dharamsala, where my chöd journey started. Almost twenty years later, two decades of researching and learning, this fascinating practice keeps my curiosity alive.

Despite the clear resemblance between the Bön and Buddhist chöd practices, so far I have not been able to locate any Buddhist or Bön account of a relationship or exchange between them with regard to this practice at the time of its origin in the eleventh and twelfth centuries. Furthermore, contemporary representatives from both sides deny that there are any historical chronicles of such connections. Neither Machig Labdrön nor Padampa Sangye are mentioned in any of the chöd sources from the Bön tradition, while the Buddhist tradition of chöd does not mention the founders of the Bön chöd, such as Milu Samlek, or its rediscoverer, a contemporary of Machig Labdrön, Guru Nontse. Yongdzin Tenzin Namdak recounts that a famous Bön treasure-discoverer, siddha, and vinaya (codes of conduct) lineage-holder by the name of Jetsun Drotsang Drugla (*Gro tsang 'brug lha*) was close friends with Padampa Sangye, and they even exchanged teachings, but there is no mention of the chöd teachings in their relationship.[256] Khetsun Sangpo Rinpoche, a renowned contemporary Tibetan Buddhist lama and historian, told me with conviction that there was no connection between the Bön and the Buddhist chöd traditions.[257] And Khetsun Sangpo is, not only a historian, but also an important Nyingma and Kagyu lama and ngakpa, who had as one of his teachers a recognized reincarnation of Machig Labdrön.

Although chöd is related to the *Perfection of Insight*, both in Bön and Buddhism, those who claim that it is the main source of chöd may be super-imposing one of the prevalent Buddhist portrayals of it and exaggerating its role. From the analysis given above, I would maintain that a "shamanic" milieu, serving as the principal matrix of the ritual's initial appearance both in Bön and Buddhism, is undeniable. Even though the use of "shamanism" as a descriptor bears only a tangential relation to one aspect of Bön (i.e., those methods under the causal vehicles, which should not to be thought by any means to be equivalent to Bön as a whole), Namkhai Norbu Rinpoche states that Machig Labdrön herself, being born into a Bönpo family, "drew from the strong shamanistic practices of this indigenous Tibetan tradition as well as from her deep knowledge of Buddhist Sutras and Tantras."[258] Thus, Machik seems to portray or embody a very special persona that incorporates her more "shamanic" background into the teachings of sutra and tantra. A persona that her disciples even to this day try to imitate: "this lifestyle is obviously conducive to the Buddhist [and Bön] ideal of nonattachment to the usual worldly concerns and possessions."[259] Norbu adds that the chöd practice "incorporates the 'self-liberation' of Dzogchen, the 'transformation' of Tantra, the gradual 'purification' of Mahāyāna-sūtra and the 'renunciation' of Hinayāna-sūtra practices."[260]

The analysis of the chöd practice in the present-day Yungdrung Bön tradition—bracketing the question of its origin—proved helpful in opening the perspectives on chöd and addressing chöd from a multivalent approach. In this way,

> images of the ancient matrix return in a reflexive manner, in terms of dialogue between diverse, interpenetrating cultural and ideological voices on a global scale.[261]

In a way it is like closing the circle and meeting the ancient matrix again, but now with a broadened perspective. The chöd from the Bön tradition expresses not just the shamanic nor the doctrines of those who are "slaves of Indic metaphysics,"[262] but "expresses an attempt to transmute this negation into a positive acceptance of ethical interindebtedness."[263] In other words, the chöd from the Bön tradition, maybe ironically, can serve as a uniting bridge between the two seemingly opposed views. Today's Yungdrung Bön religion incorporates the causal and the result vehicles in a way that does not require the practitioner to make an either-or choice. As Reynolds observes:

> The Bonpos are a refreshing exception to this [narrow sectarianism], as also was the Rimed or "non-sectarian movement" of the nineteenth century in East Tibet.[264]

And fortunately the present Dalai Lama seems to be pursuing this approach as well, continuously preaching the need for "universal responsibility," which he defines as "a deep concern for all, irrespective of creed, colour, sex, or nationality."[265] Following Mumford's schema, "the ancient matrix of interpenetration thus returns, but now in terms of the 'heteroglossia' of global communication."[266] The acceptance of all prevails against sectarian fanaticism. This may lead us to reassess the question of the nature of what is being cut (*gcod*) in the chöd practice.

In chapter 1 of *The Eight Extraordinary Chapters* by Machig Labdrön, we can read Machig Labdrön's own words regarding what is to be cut:

> As for the word 'cut', what is to be cut?
> One should cut one's attachment to the body.
> One should cut the root of one's mind.
> One should cut all directions with respect to the base.
> One should cut the taking up and casting away on the path.
> One should cut all hopes and fears about the fruit.
> If one cuts all conceptuality at all times right from where it comes up, this is known as Cutting (gCod).[267]

The different answers to the question as to what can be cut stem from the different perspectives and levels of respondents. It is important to remember that even Machig Labdrön asserts that "the devils are anything that impedes awakening into one's own nature."[268] So, even if we consider all that is to be cut as a demon, as we saw earlier, that too could refer to different things. Thus, if what is cut are the demons, in the sense of external natural forces, or illnesses in the form of malignant spirits, one could say it is a more shamanic or causal vehicles perspective; if it refers to cutting the poisons or negative emotions by means of abandoning them and acting in accordance with the *Perfection of Insight*, it is more of a sūtric view; if it refers to cutting one's defiled aggregates and transforming them into pure offerings acceptable even for the jewels of refuge, it is a tantric view; and if it refers to the cutting through the root of the thought process (*rnam rtog*), that is, cutting off the demons of self-grasping—and remaining in that nondual state, it is more of a dzogchen view. Thus the chöd practice can be seen from a multivalent approach that is even broader than what Harding's or Savvas's earlier citations expressed, one more like Norbu's, whereby the shamanic, the sūtric, the tantric, and the dzogchen views are included: "Gcod has become a pan-Tibetan individual-oriented system of religious practice that cuts across sectarian lines."[269] Chöd embraces all these philosophical views without needing to adhere to only one.

Understanding the shamanic-ritualistic or causal vehicles milieu within the chöd practice and accepting the former as a part of the latter frees ourselves from the conceptually imposed frameworks of both the ancient matrix and Buddhist philosophy. Looking at the chöd of the Bön tradition in this way—especially in relation to the chöd in the Buddhist Dzogchen tradition—can thus expand traditional horizons delimited by social boundaries, which is part and parcel of what the chöd practice itself facilitates. This third dialogic level incorporates all without leaving any view aside: no one is excluded. The Tibetan chöd truly is that which includes all, and the practitioners of it are enabled to "practice as dynamic and sophisticated agents in the context of a long-established Buddhist soteriology."[270] And as far as the efficacy of this practice, "gCod [chöd] is like taking a jet plane to Enlightenment rather than walking."[271]

Epilogue

For me this study was like looking through a keyhole. I began looking at what I thought was a very specific topic, the chöd in the Bön tradition, but this led me to see a wider spectrum. On the one hand, even though I have not found clear historical connections between the Bön and the Buddhist chöd, there is an unmistakable similarity between both traditions of chöd, and on the other hand, the chöd practice cannot be confined to only one view, as seen above.

One topic I couldn't address in this study is the connection between chöd and the representations of female aspects of reality. Although not always, it seems that in more cases than not, the deity into which the chöpa transforms is a female, a skygoer. One possible interpretation is Tenzin Wangyal Rinpoche's explanation of the female as a representation of the source. Thus, when one is freed from one's body, one returns to the oneness of the great womb, as mentioned in *Laughter of the Skygoers*. Martin's explanation of Goodwife Longexcellence's cosmogonical role in the mother tantras also reveals the importance of the feminine symbolizing the whole. Translating from the *Hyper-hermetic Sun of the Heart Tantra (Thugs kyi yang gab nyi ma'i rgyud)*, the story tells how the Female took shape from the light rays of the air and sky:

> This Female came prior to creatures and elements. Before creatures came the elements. Before elements came Shenrab. Before Shenrab came becoming. Before becoming came Sugata. Before the Sugata came Buddhahood. This female was the heart of Buddhahood. This female had good characteristics. The name she gave herself is Goodwife Longexcellence.[272]

This female aspect may be what is experienced when duality is cut off. This is not the female in opposition to the male, but the female which includes all, the source. Harding, based on metaphors from mahamudra and dzogchen, writes: "Here the mother refers to the primordial ground of being, the abiding nature of luminous awareness."[273]

Another topic that I wasn't able to pursue in this book is the connection between chöd and the funerary practice of sky burial, including the question as to which predates the other. Mumford writes: "The severance model [chöd practice], as the underlay of the Tibetan death rite, can be viewed as a transmutation of an ancient complex, incorporating themes of shamanic initiation and sacrificial exchange."[274] Martin instead, sees the two practices as codependent: "*Gcod* may be (at least in part) understood as a symbolic extension of, or possibly a psychological adaptation to, the cultural fact of corpse dismemberment."[275] Heather Stoddard also points to these similarities and is inclined to the former theory, suggesting that the popularity of chöd (and *zhi byed*) in the eleventh and twelfth centuries influenced the shift from tomb burial (in the earth) to sky burial. She also mentions possible economic reasons for this shift stemming from the collapse of the early period or *phi dar* during the tenth and eleventh centuries. Stoddard concludes that although more research is needed to establish this causal relation, "it is suggested here that both practices stand in perfect conceptual harmony with each other."[276] Thus, it would be an interesting topic to pursue.

Finally, in order to keep exploring the chöd in the Bön tradition, in the future I would like to translate the chöd of the *Secret Mother Tantra* and Shardza Rinpoche's commentary on it (and incorporate aspects of chöd that may not appear in those texts but that other chöd texts of the Bön tradition might bring forth). For now, I present here an annotated bibliography of all the chöd texts within the Bön tradition that I could find and hope that this will help others in pursuing translations of them. These may foster our understanding of the historical formation and significance of chöd in the Bön tradition and the chöd practice as a whole.

Appendix I:

The Laughter of the Skygoers (The Laughter of the Khandros [mKha' 'gro]),[277] "The Offering of the Body" from *The Great Treasury of the Ultra-profound Sky*[278]

From *The Laughter of the Khandros*, Ligmincha Institute, 2006. Reprinted by permission of Ligmincha Institute.

EXPLANATION OF THE SĀDHANA

IN *Laughter of the Khandros*, you begin the practice with **Performing the Dance**[279] of nondual view. Upon sitting down to practice, settle into the understanding that the deities and demons are mere creations of your mind—therefore there is no reason to fear them. Supported by this understanding, connect with your own strength and energy and blow the *kangling* (thighbone trumpet) to summon all the spirits and invite them to the feast. With the aid of the *damaru* (drum) and *shang* or *silnyen* (bell), abide in the state of the nonduality of emptiness and appearances and dance on the head of the demon of grasping—your mistaken belief in an existing identity or self.

In **Going for Refuge,** you take refuge in the Great Mother Satrik Yum,[280] the emptiness from which all emerges, and beseech her to embrace all sentient beings with her protection. In **Developing the Mind of Enlightenment,** you request the aid of Satrik Yum to liberate you and all the so-called gods and demons from the delusion of duality, which is the cause of harming others. With **Prayer to the Khandros,** you connect to the female deities and invoke their power to tame the harmful spirits and guide them to liberation.

In order to perform the main part of the practice, **Offering the Body,** sound *PÉ* (*phat*) and expel your consciousness upward through your central channel and out through the crown of your head. With a second *PÉ* your consciousness becomes the red-orange khandro Kalzang Ma,[281] standing in the dancing posture and adorned with bone ornaments. Your former body becomes a corpse. As Kalzang Ma you offer this corpse, which represents your ego, in two feasts or banquets: a white feast and a red feast.

Beginning with the **White Feast**, you (as Kalzang Ma) sever the cranium with the curved knife held in the right hand, chop the corpse into pieces, and place the flesh, blood, and bones inside the cranium, which becomes a cauldron (Skt. *kapala*). A short *A*, red in color, emanates from your heart to create a fire. Externally this fire melts all the elements of the physical body, which become nectar. Internally feel that the fire from the red *A* melts the upside-down white *HAM* located at the crown of your head. The resulting melted nectar fills sky and earth. Now you present this offering to the four guests. These guests are the jewels of refuge (i.e., enlightened beings), the worldly protectors, the eight classes of hindering spirits, and the beings of the six realms of existence. Having delighted the enlightened beings, you complete the two accumulations of merit and wisdom; the rejoicing protectors maintain their promise to safeguard the teachings and its practitioners; the satisfied hindering spirits become pacified; and the debts you owed to all beings of the six realms are repaid.

No one is to be excluded, and that is why there is also a **Red Feast**. Hollow out the skin and pile the corpse's flesh, bones, internal organs, and blood on it. As Yongdzin Rinpoche explains, this banquet is for the more carnivorous guests (usually among the third and fourth types of guests), who are said to arrive like vultures on a corpse. Although they are also invited to the white feast, these guests prefer the red one in which they eat the flesh, drink the blood, chew the bones, and swallow the internal organs. Eating until totally satisfied, the guests become pacified and your karmic debts of past and future lives are repaid.

Both the red and white feast offerings are boundless in that they suffice no matter how many guests come or how big their appetites are, and are infinite in that they transform into whatever the guests desire. At the end, feel that everything you have to offer has been offered and all the desires of every guest have been thoroughly satisfied.

Now that the gods and demons are totally satisfied and pacified, you present them with **The Gift of Bön**, requesting them to cause no further harm to others and instead to take refuge and develop the mind of enlightenment, or bodhicitta. **The Gift of Protection** is to prompt the recognition of their own true nature as buddhas, or enlightened beings. These are the teachings of the nature of mind.

Finally, with the **Prayer and Dedication**, you dedicate the merit of the practice to those gods and demons who have created obstacles as well as to all sentient beings, with the wish that all will attain enlightenment.

TRANSLATION OF THE SĀDHANA

INTRODUCTION

I pay homage to the knowledge holders, khandros, and deities.[282]
In order to accomplish the intention and conduct of the khandros
This illusory body is circulated as a wheel of offering.
Begin by going to a fearful place and taming the land.
The yogi who realizes the equality of samsara and nirvana
Sings the song and dances the dance of playful primordial wisdom.
Together with the sounds of the drum and bell—the inseparability of
　　method and insight—
[This yogi] chants the following words which well up from the state
　　of selflessness:

THE PRACTICE

Performing the Dance
Even though so-called gods and demons appear here,
They were created from nothing other than the vastness of the
　　Great Mother's womb or vagina (Sanskrit: *bhaga*)
The unceasing dynamic energy of the base becomes the dance
　　of self-appearance,
Which naturally dissolves into nondual primordial wisdom.
　　YA LA LA!
[I] dance upon the heads of these wild demons of grasping at duality
And upon the corpse of the great demon of grasping at a self,
　　destroying them.
My song of natural egolessness draws them into space.
Leaping into the sky, I gesture and dance, creating a magical display,

And with the lion's roar of emptiness, this yogi
Shatters the skulls of these foxes, these male and female hindering
     demons.[283]
With my dance of the play of great bliss and primordial wisdom,
I pulverize dualistic self-clinging and emotional afflictions.
HUNG HUNG HUNG PÉ PÉ PÉ

Going for Refuge

O Mother, Satrik Yum, you are the uncontrived base, the great
     emptiness.
I go for refuge in the vast space of the Great Mother.
O Mother, please regard with your compassion all gods and demons
     of this untamed, frightening place
As well as the sentient beings of the six realms, all who have been my
     mother.
PÉ

Developing the Mind of Enlightenment (Skt. Bodhicitta)

Through delusion, unknowing, and self-grasping,
These demons have caused harm to other sentient beings.
Now, having realized the mind of enlightenment
May these beings be liberated within the primordially pure space.
PÉ

Prayer to the Khandros[284]

E MA HO!

How marvelous! I pray to the body of truth, Kuntu Zangmo.
I pray to the body of perfection, Sherab Parchin.
I pray to the Great Mother Chema Ötso.
I pray to the khandro Kalpa Zangmo.
I pray to the khandro Tukjé Kündröl.
I pray to the khandro Öden Nyibar.
I pray to the khandro Sipé Gyalmo.
I pray to the white peaceful khandros.
I pray to the green increasing khandros.
I pray to the red powerful khandros.

I pray to the blue wrathful khandros.

I pray to the four classes of terrifying gatekeeper goddesses.

I pray to my kind root master.

May the overflowing dynamic energy of the intention of these hosts
of mothers

Subdue the gods and demons of this untamed, frightening place,

Vanquish the gods and demons of this untamed, frightening place,

And guide all the unrealized sentient beings of the three worlds into
space!

O sole Mother, having been mixed into a single mass of space,

PÉ

May all beings without exception achieve perfect buddhahood!

PÉ

Offering the Body

(Literally: [My] consciousness flies upward and is liberated from my
physical body).

My unborn mind abandons this body and self-grasping,

Expelled into the sky through the path of the central channel.

PÉ

I arise in a rainbow display as Kalzang Ma, destroyer of the demons of
conflicting emotions,

In a dancing posture, adorned with the six [bone] ornaments.[285]

PÉ

White Feast

With the curved knife in her right hand, she liberates the demon
of the aggregates.[286]

She cuts off the head of that arrogant demon.

The severed skull is placed as a cauldron as vast as the three-thousand-
fold universe.[287]

The physical aggregates of my abandoned body are flung into
the vessel.

The heart's secret treasure emanates a short *A*

Whose fire dissolves the aggregate of form.

Thus the physical body's constituents and elements melt into nectar.[288]

By the drops of the refined nectar from *A* and *HAM*,[289]
This nectar of one hundred flavors fills sky and earth.[290]
PÉ
To the source of refuge, the three precious jewels, I make
    this offering.
To the hosts of protectors of the sacred teachings, accept
    [this offering] and be pleased.
To the eight classes of obstructing beings and elementals, enjoy
    [this offering] and be content.
To the beings of the six realms, our mothers, partake of this
    offering and be satisfied.[291]
PÉ
Through pleasing the divine guests with this offering, may the two
    accumulations be perfected.
By delighting the protectors of the teachings of Bön, may their
    oath-bound commitments be upheld.
May all harm and adversity caused by malevolent male and female
    demons be pacified,
[And] through satisfying the wishes of our mothers, all sentient
    beings, may all karmic debts be repaid.
PÉ PÉ PÉ

Red Feast
With the curved knife in her right hand, she liberates the demon
    of the aggregates.
Cutting off the head of this arrogant demon, atop its flayed skin
    the size of the three-thousandfold universe,
She heaps the flesh and blood.
Like vultures feasting on the remains of a corpse,
The gods and demons of this frightful place gather.
May those who desire flesh tear it with their teeth and eat!
May those who desire blood drink it gulp by gulp!
May those who desire bones gnaw the bones and suck the marrow![292]
Pull out the organs and entrails and feast upon them!
Thus may my karmic debts of [this and] previous lifetimes
    be repaid,

[And] may the negative intentions of these malevolent demons
be pacified.
PÉ PÉ PÉ

The Gift of Bön

Gods and demons who dwell in this great secret place,
Abandon forever the mind of harming others!
Take refuge in the four yungdrung (lamas, buddhas, shenrabs, and
bön—or dharma).[293]
Generate compassion for all sentient beings, our mothers.
PÉ

The Gift of Protection

In cutting the root of the thinker of thoughts and memory,
Ultimately, it is vividly clear that there are no entities.
This is the pure understanding of Kun[tu] Zang[po].
Now, recognizing one's own natural face, may all be liberated!
PÉ

Prayer and Dedication

The virtue arising from this great stainless accumulation
I dedicate [for the benefit] of the gods and demons of this untamed,
frightening place.
From the richness of the treasury of the two accumulations,
May all beings equally and spontaneously attain buddhahood.
PÉ

*The sādhana was translated by the Ligmincha Translation Committee. The
translation greatly benefited from the work of an earlier translation by John
Myrdhin Reynolds. May the guardians forgive any errors that we may have
introduced. The practice is intended for use by those who have received transmission and explanation from an authentic lineage holder. Please respect
this request. Our heartfelt gratitude to our teachers! May our teachers enjoy
excellent health and long life! May their dharma activities flourish! May all
beings benefit!*

[Colophon]

This is sealed with the nonobjectifying of the three wheels [agent, action, and that which is acted upon].[294] My own ordained disciple from Nyaq Tsun [Nyag Rong] whose name is Prājña, requested me to write the above. [He did so] with the second [kind of] jewels [i.e., silver coins][295] and flowers, extending a pure clean scarf (*lha dar*)[296] to me, Shardza Chadrel Rigpa Rangshar (*Shar rdza'i bya bral rig pa rang shar*). Through the virtues of writing this text, may all mother sentient beings obtain complete enlightenment.

Sarva Mangalam. Tashi So.

Tibetan Folios of the
The Laughter of the Skygoers
see following pages

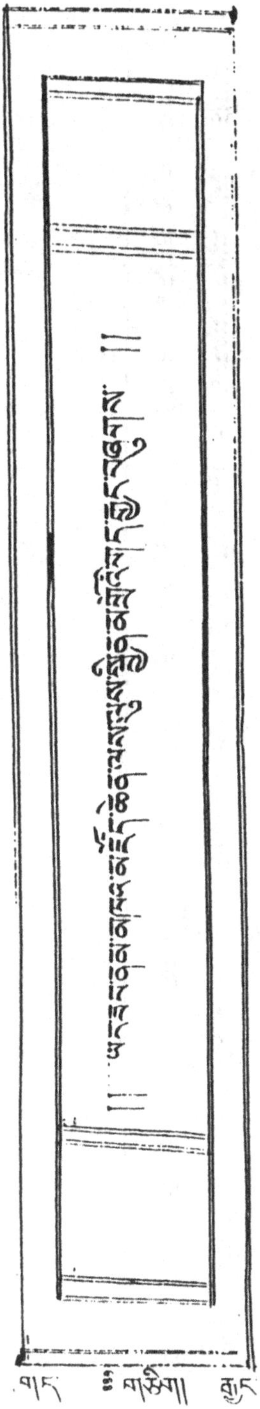

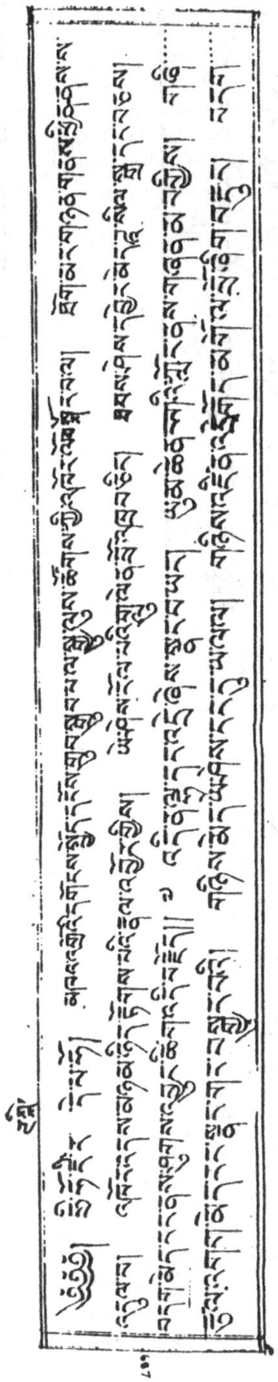

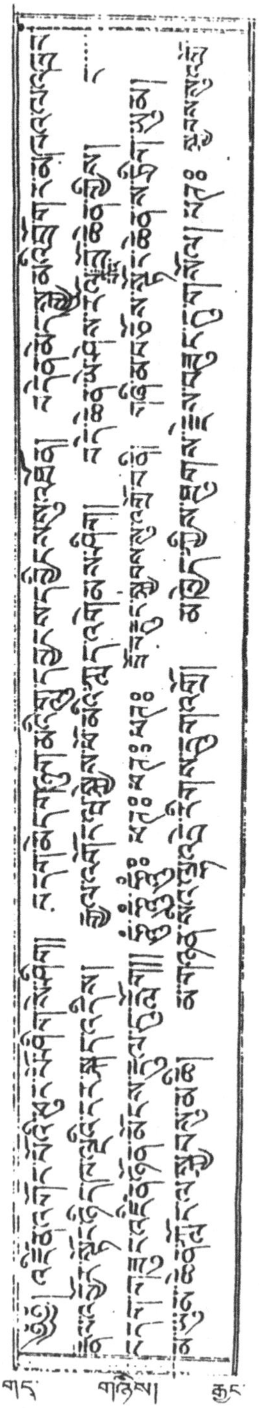

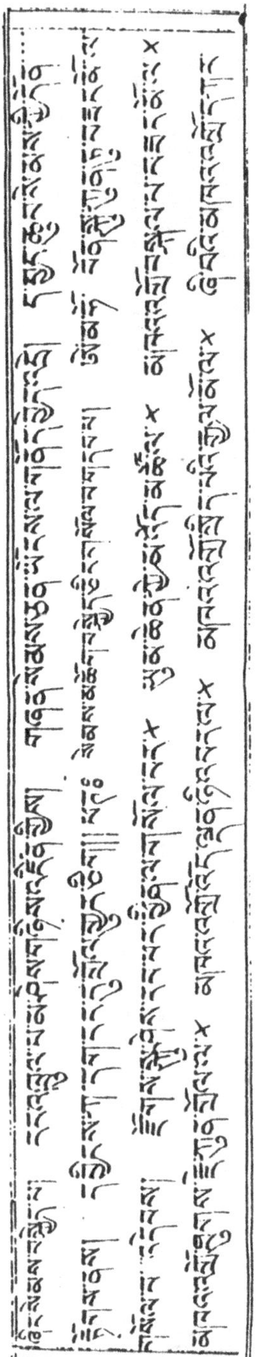

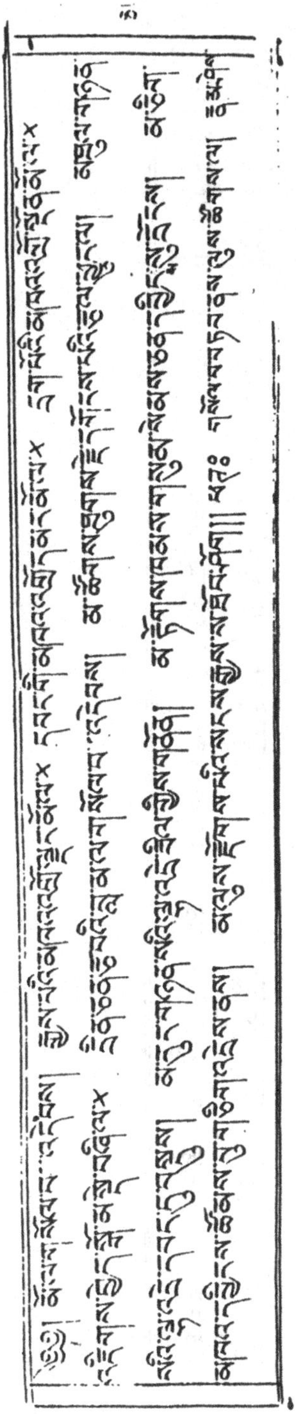

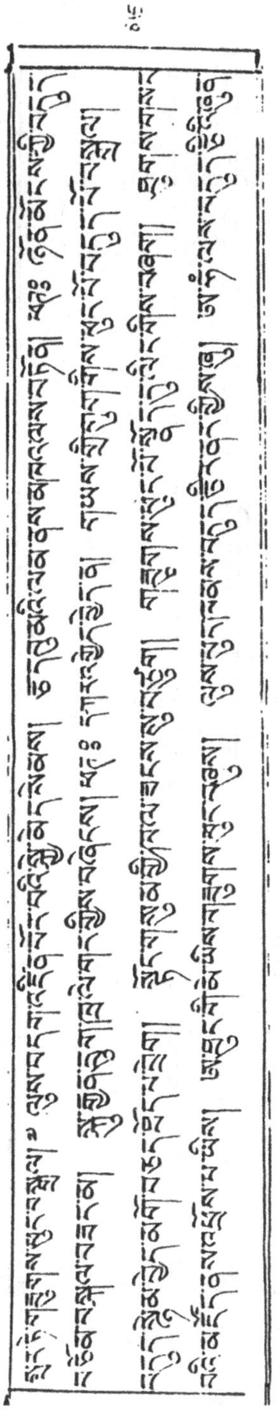

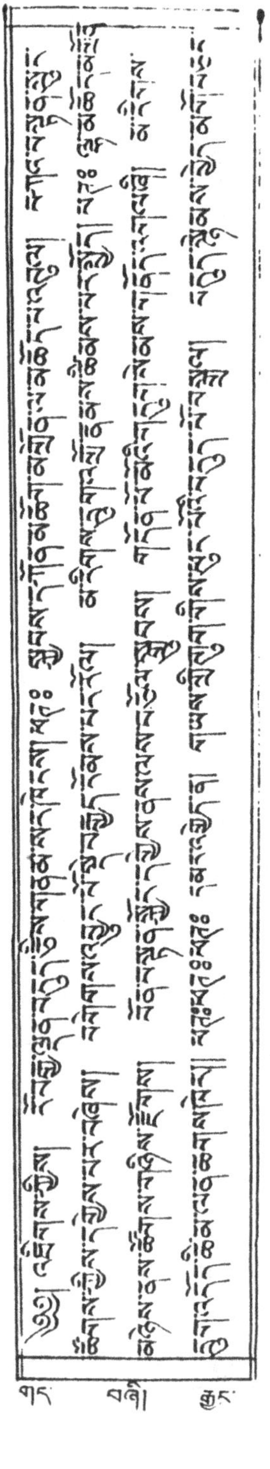

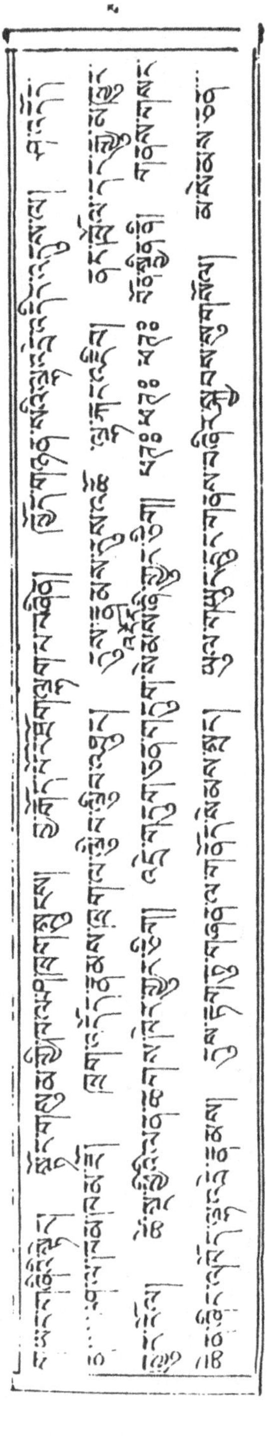

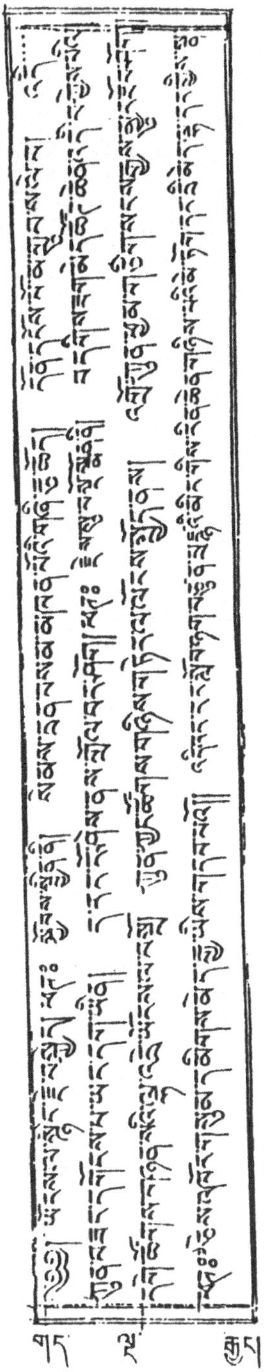

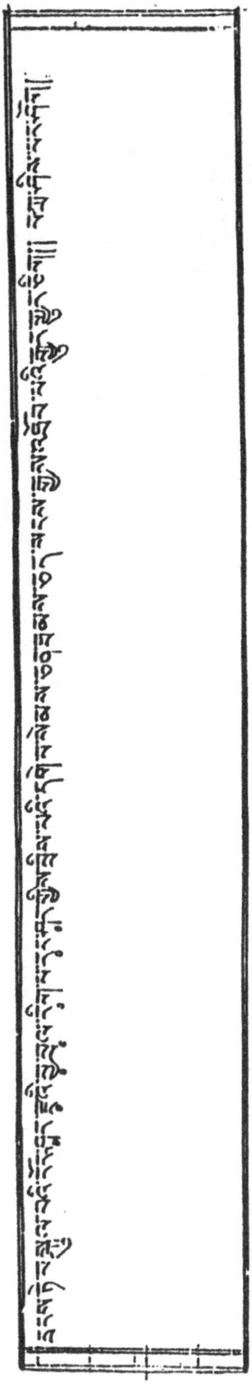

Appendix II:

Secret Mother Tantra Index *(dkar chags)*

This index was created and handwritten by Geshe Lungrig Namgyal
from Tritsan Norbutse Monastery.

ཨྠ྅༑༑ མ་རྒྱུད་གསང་བ་ལམ་ཁྱེར་གྱི་འགྲེལ་བའི་

དཀར་ཆགས།

ཕྱེར་ནུ་

མཚོད་བརྗོད་དང་ལམ་རྒྱག་བསྐོམ་ལམ་ཆོ་ག་ཐུག ཉེ་དབང་པོ་རྒྱ་དང་སྐྱོར་རྒྱལ། ①

P. 656

ཆོགས་ཀྱི་ཐིག་ལེ་ཡེ་ཤེས་རྒྱུའི་ལ་རྟོགས། འདི་ རྫ་ལ་རོན་ལུ་སྟེ། ཆོགས་ཆེན་རྩ་མ་ལ་
བསྐྱབ་པ་དང་། ཐིག་ལེ་རིག་གཅིག་ཏུ་བཅད་པ་དང་། ཡེ་ཤེས་གཉན་ཆོག་ཏུ་དབབ་པ་དང་།
རྒྱུབ་པའི་རྣད་གདོན་གཅོད་པ་དང་། རྟོགས་པའི་དོན་ཆིད་བསྟན་པའི། 657

དང་པོ་ཆོགས་ཆེན་རྩ་མ་ལ་བསྐྱབ་པ་ལ་གསུམ་སྟེ། ཆོགས་གནས་གཉན་པོ་བགྲོད་ད་དང་།
ཆོགས་ཆེན་ཆནས་མེད་བཀྱེ་བ་དང་། རྒྱ་མ་མཛོན་འགྱུར་བསྐྱབ་པའི།། 657

དང་པོ་ཆོགས་གནས་གཉན་པོ་བགྲོད་པ། | 657

གཉིས་པ་ཐོབ་པ་མེན་རྣམས་ཁེན་ཟཏེ་པོ་ལ་བའི་ 658

གསུམ་པ་སྐྱ་མ་བཏོན་འགྱུར་ལ་ཆཐབ་པ་ལ་གསུམ། 660

སྒྱེ་དོན་གཉིས་པ་ཐེག་མི་ནག་གཐེག་ཏུ་བཆད་པ་ 664

སྐྱེ་དོན་གསུམ་པ་ཡེ་ཤེས་ཐབ་ཆོག་ཏུ་དཐབ་པ་ལ་གསུམ། 667

དང་པོ་ཡེ་ཤེས་གཉན་ཆོག་ཏུ་དཐབ། 667

གཉིས་པ་གཉན་ཆོག་ཏུ་གཉན་དཐབ་པ། 667

གསུམ་པ་ནཉར་ཆེན་ཁར་ལ་གཏད་པ། 668

སྐྱེ་དོན་ཐཐི་པ་རྒྱབ་པཐི་ཉད་གདོན་པཐད་པཐི་   ཐཐས་ལ་གསུམ་ཐེ།

དཐེགས་པ་དེུར་དི་འཛིར་རྱི་གཉན་ཆོག་གཉན་དཐབ་པ་དང་།

སྒྱོད་ལཐ་ཀྱི་གཉན་ཆོག་གཉར་དཐབ་པ་དང་།

ལུ་ཐཆོས་རྟོག་གསུམ་འཐཐ་ཏུ་བཐི་སྒྱུར་ཆྱིད་བཆོ། 670 ----

སྐྱེ་དོན་...ལུ་པ་རྟོགས་པཐི་དོན་ཆིད་ཐཐུན་པ་ལ་གསུམ་ཐེ། 673

རྟོགས་པཐི་དོད་ཆིད་ཆོས་ཐཐུད་ཐ་དད། 674

ཐིར་མི་ལྱོ་པཐི་ནོ་ཐཆོ་ཐ་དད། 677

ཡོན་ནོ་གཉད་ཏུ་གཉེར་ཐཐང་ཐཆོ། 679

Appendix III:
Annotated Bibliography of Chöd Texts
from the Bön Tradition

This bibliography of Bön chöd texts provides the available information on each text. In each category, the texts are in listed in historical order, earliest text first. The information is provided in the following order: title; author and mode of authorship (i.e., composed, rediscovered, or received transmission); a general description of its contents; information about publication and origin, when available.

MOTHER TANTRA

Ma rgyud sangs rgyas rgyud gsum rtsa 'grel.
The Three Basic [Secret] Mother Tantras with Commentaries. Kuntu Zangpo is considered to be the author of the Root Texts, and Milu Samlek (*rGyal gShen Mi Lus bSam Legs*) of the Commentaries. Terma (*gter ma*) rediscovered by Guru Nontse (*Gu ru rnon rtse*). It also includes a later text: *mKhan chen nyi ma rgyal mtshan gyi gsang mchog gi dbang lung thob tshul,* by Mushen Nyima Gyaltsen (*dMu gshen nyi ma rgyal mtshan,* b. 1360), which describes the transmission of this teaching through its lineage-holders. Chöd is found in chapter *kha,* the Root Text of the Path, and in its Commentary, chapter *tsha.* Reproduced from original manuscript belonging to the Monastery of Samling (*bSam gling*), in Dolpo, N.W. Nepal. Dolanji, India: Bonpo Monastic Centre, distributor, 1971.

Ma rgyud thugs rje nyi ma'i rgyud skor.
The [Secret] Mother Tantra: The Tantric Cycle of the Sun of Compassion. Authorship and mode of composition same as above. Chöd is found in chapter 2, the Root Text of the Path, and in its Commentary, chapter 20.

Ed. by Tshultrim Tashi. Reproduced from a rare manuscript recently found in the Monastery of Shendar Ding Rigyal (*gShen dar lding ri rgyal*). Dolanji, India: Tibetan Bonpo Monastic Community, 1985.

Ral gri phyung rdeg.
Composed by Mushen Nyima Gyaltsen (*dMu gshen nyi ma rgyal mtshan*) in the fourteenth century. A commentary with a sādhana of the chöd practice of the *Secret Mother Tantra*. Text not available to me at this time.

gSang sngags ma rgyud gnyan sa lam khyer gyi gcod kyi khrid yig bdud bzhi tshar gcod.
Composed by Shardza Tashi Gyaltsen (*Shar rdza bkhra shis rgyal mtshan,* 1859–1934). A commentary on the chöd practice of the *Secret Mother Tantra.* The block-printed copy has no date of publication or publisher.

gSang ba sang chen ma rgyud rgyal ba rgya mtsho'i gnyan sa lam 'khyer gyi gdam ba gsang ba'i rgya can.
Composed by Shardza Tashi Gyaltsen (*Shar rdza bkhra shis rgyal mtshan,* 1859–1934). A sādhana of the chöd practice of the *Secret Mother Tantra.* The block-printed copy has no date of publication or publisher.

PEACEFUL CHÖD

A dkar zhi gcod.
Received in a visionary experience transmission from Khandro Karmo Chenchig (*mKhan 'gro dkar mo chen gcig,* Great White Lady Skygoer) by Marton Gyalek (*Mar ston rgyal legs*) alias *sMan gong ba,* born in 1062 in Tsongnyan Mengkong (*mTsho snya sman gong ba*)—North of Shigatse—in the Tibetan area of Tsang (*gTsang*). It was obtained by Yongdzin Tenzin Namdak Rinpoche during his visit to Tibet in 1986.[297] It is not yet published.

EXTENDING CHÖD

Zab lam gnad kyi gdams pa drug mu gcod chen gyi gsung pod.
Received by Shense Lhaje (*gShen gsas lha rje,* fl. 1310, b. 1215) alias Golde

Phagpa Yungdrung Yeshe (*Go lde 'phags pa gyung drung ye shes*) and Nyo Nyima Sherab (*gNyos nyi ma shes rab*) in a visionary experience transmission of the teachings of Tongyung Tuchen (*sTong rgyung mthu chen*). A collection of Bön chöd tantras (*rgyud*), rituals (*cho ga*), and instructions (*khrid yig*). Reproduced from a manuscript preserved at Samling Monastery. Edited by Tsultrim Tashi. New Thobgyal: Tibetan Bonpo Monastic Centre, 1973.

gCod gdams kyi skor.
Received by Shense Lhaje (*gShen gsas lha rje*, fl. 1310, b. 1215) but in this case under the name of Drumu Hara (*Drun mu ha ra*) alias Yungdrung Odzer (*g. Yung drung 'od zer*), in a visionary experience of the teachings of Tongyung Tuchen. An ancient Bön cycle of chöd practice. Reproduced from an old manuscript in Samling Monastery. Edited by Tshultrim Tashi. Dolanji: Tibetan Bonpo Monastic Centre, 1985.

POWERFUL CHÖD

Zab lam mkha' 'gro gsang ba'i gcod kyi gdams pa.
"The Profound Path of Chöd Instructions of the Secret Skygoers." Oral transmission received by Tulku Tronyen Gyaltsen (*sPrul sku khro gnyan rgyal mtshan*, fourteenth century).[298] A collection of Bön chöd tantras and related texts. Reproduced from a manuscript preserved at Samling (*bSam gling*) Monastery in Dolpo, N.W. Nepal. Edited by Tashi Dorji. Dolanji: Tibetan Bonpo Monastic Centre, 1973.

mKha' 'gro gsang gcod yid bzin nor bu'i chos skor.
Oral transmission received by Tulku Tronyen Gyaltsen (*sPrul sku khro gnyan rgyal mtshan*, fourteenth century), with supplementary texts by later Bön masters. A system of practice of the *mKha' 'gro gsang gcod* cycle. Reproduced from a rare manuscript from the library of the late Sherab Dragpa (*Shes rab grags pa*) of Chugtsho (*Phyug 'tsho*) Monastery of Tago (*rTa sgo*) in Tibet. Dolanji: Tibetan Bonpo Monastic Centre, 1985.

mKha' 'gro gsang gcod kyi lag len skor.
Cycle of Chöd Practices of the Secret Skygoers. Received by Kyangtrul Namkha Gyaltsen (*sKyang sprul nam mkha' rgyal mtshan,* fl. 1770),[299] in a vision-

ary experience of the teachings of Tronyan Gyaltsen. Texts outlining various practices of the Bön chöd precepts from the *mKha' 'gro gsang gcod* cycle. Reproduced from a rare manuscript collection from Chadur (*Bya du*r) in Tibet. Edited by Tashi Dorje. Dolanji: Tibetan Bonpo Monastic Centre, 1974.

mKha' 'gro gsang gcod yid bzin nor bu'i dmigs pa'i skor rnams cha tshang.
Kyangtrul Namkha Gyaltsen (*sKyang sprul nam mkha' rgyal mtshan*, fl. 1770). Teachings of the *mKha' 'gro gsang gcod* cycle. Reproduced from manuscripts preserved at Dorpatan Monastery in Nepal. Edited by Gelong Sonam Gyaltsen. Dolanji: Tibetan Bonpo Monastic Centre, 1974.

WRATHFUL CHÖD

Zab mo gcod kyi gdams nag yum chen thugs rje sgrol ma.
"Profound Instructions on Chöd, called *Liberation through Yum Chenmo's Compassion.*" Terma rediscovered by Nagter Sangngag Lingpa (*Nag gter gsang sngangs gling pa*, b. 1864) alias Walchung Terchen (*dBal chung gter chen*). Reproduced from a collection of Delhi lithographic prints published by Khyuntrul Jigme Namkhai Dorje (*Khyun sprul 'jig med nam mkha'i rdo rje*) about 1955. Edited by Patshang Lama Sonam Gyaltsen. New Thobgyal: Tibetan Bonpo Monastic Centre, 1973.

bYams ma'i snin thig.
Terma rediscovered by Nagter Sangngag Lingpa (*Nag gter gsang sngangs gling pa*, b. 1864) alias Walchung Terchen (*dBal chung gter chen*). A cycle of New Bön (*bon gsar*) chöd practice. Reproduced from a rare manuscript brought from Tibet. Edited by Tinley Jatso. Dehra Dun, Uttar Pradesh, 1985.

Rol pa zan thal gyi gcod skor.
Terma rediscovered by Nagter Sangngag Lingpa (*Nag gter gsang sngangs gling pa*, b. 1864) alias Walchung Terchen (*dBal chung gter chen*), with liturgical annotations and comments by Patshan Lama Nima Bumsel (*sPa tshan bla ma ni ma 'bum g sal*). A cycle of New Bön chöd practice. Reproduced from a rare manuscript from Patshan Labran (*sPa tshan bla bran*). Dolanji: Tibetan Bonpo Monastic Centre, 1985.

Yum chen ma 'od mtsho'i zab gsang gcod kyi gdams pa las phran dang bcas pa'i gsung pod.
Terma rediscovered by Khandro Dechen Wangmo (*mKha' 'gro bde chen dbang mo*, b. 1868). A collection of New Bön chöd precepts. Reproduced from a manuscript brought from Kongpo (*Kong po*) in SE Tibet, where it was preserved in the well-known New Bön monastery of Gyalri (*rGyal ri*) or Jeri (*rJe ri*). Edited by Tshering Wangyal. Dolanji: Tibetan Bonpo Monastic Centre, 1974.

OTHER

Tshe dban bod yul ma.
Rediscovered by Bonzig Yungdrung Lingpa (*Bon dzig g.yung drung glin pa*, b. 1228), also known as Dorje Lingpa (*rDo rje ling pa*). A dzogchen cycle of life consecration precepts, ritual, and meditation instructions linked to the oral transmission of Tsewang Rigzin (*Tshe dban rig 'dzin*). Copied from a blockprint from Hor Bontha (*Hor bon tha*) belonging to Yongdzin Tenzin Namdak. Edited by Yungdrung Gyaltsen (*g.Yung drung rgyal mtshan*). Delhi: Tibetan Bonpo Monastic Centre, 1973.

dPa'i bo bdun pa.
Terma rediscovered by Mishig Dorje (*Mi shig rdo rje*) alias Yungdrung Gyalpo (*g.Yun drung rgyal po*, b. 1650). Also linked to the oral transmission of Tsewang Rigzin. This text also has instructions on how to stop hail as part of the chöpa's practice. Text not available to me at this time.

Yang zab nam mkha' mdzod chen le lus sbyin mkha' 'gro'i gad rgyang.
Composed by Shardza Tashi Gyaltsen. A brief chöd sādhana belonging to the collection known as *Treasure of the Profound Sky* (*Nam mkha' mdzod*), in which there are several ritual texts and works of the four initiations (*dbang bzhi*). This chöd sādhana appears in the second of three volumes in which this collection is printed (it also includes other ritual texts from the *rDzogs chen sku gsum rang shar*). Reproduced from examples of the Delhi lithographic edition of the early 1950s and xylographic prints from the Eastern region of Kham. Edited by Ngawang Sonam, Patshang Lama Sonam

Gyaltsen, and Khedup Gyatso. New Thobgyal: Tibetan Bonpo Monastic Centre, 1974. Vol. 1 was printed in 1973, and Vol. 3 in 1973–74).

gSang ba yeshes.
Composed by Kyundrol Zhaton Nyingpo (*Kyun grol gzha'i tshon snying po*, seventeenth century). A cycle of New Bön chöd practice. Text not available to me at this time.

Selected Bibliography

Dorje, Rinjing, and Ter Ellingson. 1979. "Explanation of the Secret Gcod Damaru: An Exploration of Musical Instrument Symbolism." *Asian Music* 10, no. 2: 63–91.

Dreyfus, George. 2003. *The Sound of Two Hands Clapping: The Education of a Tibetan Buddhist Monk*. Berkeley: University of California Press.

Edou, Jerome. 1996. *Machig Labdrön and the Foundations of Chöd*. Ithaca, NY: Snow Lion Publications.

Ermakov, Dimitri. 2008. *Bo and Bon: Ancient Shamanic Traditions of Siberia and Tibet and Their Relation to the Teachings of a Central Asian Buddhism*. Kathmandu: Vajra Publications.

Evans-Wentz, W. Y. 1935. *Tibetan Yoga and Secret Doctrines*. London: Oxford University Press. Reprinted 1958.

Germano, David. 1994. *Dzogchen Mini-Encyclopaedia*. Charlottesville: University of Virginia. Booklet.

Gyaltsen, Tronyan Tulku (*sPrul sku khro gnyan rgyal mtshan*). 1973. *Zab lam mkha' 'gro gsan ba'i gcod kyi gdams pa*. Ed. Tashi Dorji. New Thobgyal, India: Tibetan Bonpo Monastic Centre.

Gyatso, Janet. 1985. "The Development of the *Gcod* Tradition." In *Soundings in Tibetan Civilization*, ed. Barbara Aziz and Matthew Kapstein, 320–41. Delhi: Manohar.

His Holiness the Fourteenth Dalai Lama of Tibet. "A Human Approach to World Peace." The Office of His Holiness the Dalai Lama. http://www.dalailama.com/page.62.htm.

Huber, Toni. 1994. "Putting the *gnas* Back into *gnas-skor*: Rethinking Tibetan Buddhist Pilgrimage Practice." *Tibet Journal* 19, no. 2: 23–60.

Jones, Annette Lucy. 1998. "Transgressive Compassion: The Role of Fear, Horror, and the Threat of Death in Ultimate Transformation." PhD diss., Rice University.

Karmay, Samten, ed. and trans. 1972. *The Treasury of Good Sayings: A Tibetan History of Bon*. London: Oxford University Press.

———. 1975. "A General Introduction to the History and Doctrines of Bon." In *Memoirs of the Research Department of the Toyo Bunko* 33: 171–218.

———. 1977. *A Catalogue of Bonpo Publications*. Tokyo: The Toyo Bunko.

Klein, Anne C., and Geshe Tenzin Wangyal Rinpoche. 2006. *Unbounded Wholeness: Dzogchen, Bon, and the Logic of the Nonconceptual*. Oxford: Oxford University Press.

Kvaerne, Per. 1994. "The Bon Religion of Tibet: A Survey of Research." In *Buddhist Forum*, Vol. 3, ed. T. Skorupski and U. Pagel, 131–41. London: School of Oriental and African Studies, University of London.

———. 1996. *The Bon Religion of Tibet: The Iconography of a Living Tradition*. Boston: Shambhala.

Leithauser, Brad. 1994. *The Norton Book of Ghost Stories*. New York: W. W. Norton and Company.

Lhaje, Shense (*gShen gsas lha rje*). 1973. *Zab lam gnad kyi gdams pa drug mu gcod chen gyi gsu pod*, ed. Tsultrim Tashi. New Thobgyal: Tibetan Bonpo Monastic Centre.

Lingpa, Nyagter Sangngak (*Nyag gter gsang sngags gling pa*), discoverer. 1973. *Zab mo gcod kyi gdams nag yum chen thugs rje sgrol ma*, ed. Patshang Lama Sonam Gyaltsen. New Thobgyal: Tibetan Bonpo Monastic Centre.

Lopez, Donald S., Jr. 1988. *Elaborations on Emptiness: Uses of the Heart Sutra*. Princeton: Princeton University Press.

Martin, Dan. 1991. "The Emergence of Bon and the Tibetan Polemical Tradition." PhD diss., Indiana University.

———. 1994. *Mandala Cosmogony: Human Body Good Thought and the Revelation of the Secret Mother Tantras of Bon*. Wiesbaden: Harrassowitz Verlag.

———. 1996. "On the Cultural Ecology of Sky Burial on the Himalayan Plateau." *East and West* (Rome) 46, nos. 3-4: 353–70.

Mimaki, Katsumi. 1994a. "Doxographie tibétaine et classifications indiennes." In *Actes du colloque franco-japonais de septembre 1991*, ed. Fumimasa Fukui and Gérard Fussman. Paris: École française d'Extrême-Orient.

_____. 1994b. "A Fourteenth-Century Bon Po Doxography: The *Bon sgo byed* by Tre ston rgyal mtshan dpal—A Preliminary Report toward a Critical Edition." In *Proceedings of the 6th Seminar of the International Association of Tibetan Studies, Fagernes 1992*, Vol. 2., ed. P. Kvaerne, 570–79. Oslo: Institute for Comparative Research in Human Culture.

Mumford, Stan Royal. 1989. *Himalayan Dialogue: Tibetan Lamas and Gurung Shamans in Nepal.* Madison: University of Wisconsin Press.

Nebesky-Wojkowitz, René de. 1993. *Oracles and Demons of Tibet: The Cult and Iconography of the Tibetan Protective Deities.* Kathmandu: Tiwari's Pilgrims Book House.

Norbu, Namkhai. 1981. *The Necklace of gZi: A Cultural History of Tibet.* Dharamsala: Narthang Publications.

_____. 1986. *The Crystal and the Way of Light.* Ed. John Shane. New York: Routledge and Kegan Paul.

_____. 1991. *The Dzogchen Ritual Practices.* Ed. and trans. Brian Beresford. London: Kailash Editions.

_____. 1995. *Drung, Deu, and Bon: Narrations, Symbolic Languages, and the Bön Tradition in Ancient Tibet.* Trans. A. Clemente and A. Lukianowicz. Dharamsala: Library of Tibetan Works and Archives.

Ohnuma, Reiko. 1997. "Dedhāna and the Buddhist Conceptions of the Body." PhD diss., University of Wisconsin.

Orofino, Giacomella. 1987. *Contributo allo studio dell' insegnamento di Ma gcig Lab sgron.* Supplemento 53 agli Annali, vol. 47. Napoli: Istituto Universitario Orientale.

_____. 1990. "The State of the Art in the Study on the Zhang zhung Language." *Annali* 50, fasc. 1, 83–85. Napoli: Istituto Universitario Orientale.

_____. 2000. "The Great Wisdom Mother and the Gcod Tradition." In *Tantra in Practice*, ed. D. G. White, 398–416. Princeton: Princeton University Press.

Reynolds, John Myrdhin. 1991. *Yungdrung Bon, The Eternal Tradition: The Ancient Pre-Buddhist Religion of Central Asia and Tibet: Its History, Teachings, and Literature.* Freehold, NJ: Bonpo Translation Project. Booklet.

_____. 1993. *The Mother Tantra from the Bon Tradition.* San Diego: Bonpo Translation Project/Bonpo Research Foundation. Booklet.

―――. 1996a. *The Practice of Chod in the Bon Tradition*. San Diego: Vidyadhara Publications. Booklet.

―――. 1996b. *The Threefold Practice of the Primordial State of the Mother Tantra*. San Diego: Vidyadhara Publications. Booklet.

―――. 1996c. *The Mandala of the Sun*. San Diego: Bonpo Translation Project. Booklet.

Samlek, Miluk. 1971. *Mother Tantra. Ma rgyud sangs rgyas rgyud gsum rtsa 'grel* (The Three Basic Mother Tantras with Commentaries). Delhi: Tibetan Bonpo Monastic Centre.

―――. 1985. *Ma rgyud thugs rje nyi ma'i rgyud skor.* Ed. Tashi Tshultrim. Dolanji, India: Tibetan Bonpo Monastic Community.

Samuel, Geoffrey. 1990. *Mind, Body, and Culture: Anthropology and the Biological Interface*. New York: Cambridge University Press.

―――. 1993. *Civilized Shamans: Buddhism in Tibetan Societies*. Washington: Smithsonian Institution Press.

―――. 2005a. *Tantric Revisionings*. New Delhi: Motilal Banarsidas and Ashgate.

―――. 2005b. "Shamanism, Bon, and Tibetan Religion." In *Tantric Revisionings*, 116–137. New Delhi: Motilal Banarsidas and Ashgate.

―――. 2008. *The Origins of Yoga and Tantra: Indic Religions to the Thirteenth Century*. London: Cambridge University Press.

Śāntideva. 1996. *The Bodhicaryāvatāra*. Trans. Kate Crosby and Andrew Skilton. Oxford: Oxford University Press.

Savvas, Carol Diane. 1990. "A Study of the Profound Path of *Gcod*: The Mahāyāna Buddhist Meditation Tradition of Tibet's Great Woman Saint Machig Labdron." PhD diss., University of Wisconsin.

Snellgrove, David. 1967. *The Nine Ways of Bon*. London: Oxford University Press.

Tucci, Giuseppe. 1988. *The Religions of Tibet*. Trans. Geoffrey Samuel. Berkeley: University of California Press.

Yungdrung, Drugyelwa (*Bru chen rgyal ba gyung drung*). 1994. *The Experiential Transmission of Drugyelwa Yungdrung*, Part 1. Trans. David Germano. Charlottesville, VA: Ligmincha Institute.

Zhonupal, Go Lotsawa (*Gos lo tsāba gZhon nu dpal*). 1995. *Blue Annals*. Trans. George Roerich. Delhi: Motilal Banarsidass Publishers. First edition, Calcutta, 1949.

Notes

Acknowledgments

1 At an earlier stage of his life, Yongdzin Tenzin Namdak Rinpoche was known as Lopon Tenzin Namdak, but so as not to confuse the reader, I will always refer to him by his current title, Yongdzin Tenzin Namdak.

2 The panel was titled "Origin and Development of the Zhi byed and gCod Traditions in the Cultural History of Tibet." Other presenters in that panel were Michelle Sorensen, Elena De Rossi Filibeck, and Monika Roenning. My gratitude goes to all the presenters, and in particular to Giacomella Orofino for organizing, presiding over, and presenting at this panel.

Introduction: Enchanted by the Melody

3 This is a Sanskrit word, also adopted by the Tibetans, for a two-sided drum which is used in the chöd practice.

4 This study will use Mikhail Bakhtin's model of "dialogic" interaction, mainly from his *The Dialogical Imagination*, trans. C. Emerson and M. Holquist (Austin: University of Texas Press, 1981) as presented in Stan Royal Mumford, *Himalayan Dialogue: Tibetan Lamas and Gurung Shamans in Nepal* (Madison: University of Wisconsin Press, 1989).

5 Mumford 1989, 16.

Chöd: Offering One's Body

6 Namkhai Norbu, *The Crystal and the Way of Light*, ed. John Shane (New York: Routledge and Kegan Paul, 1986), 49.

7 W. Y. Evans-Wentz, *Tibetan Yoga and Secret Doctrines* (London: Oxford University Press, 1935), 282. Evans-Wentz was the first, to my knowledge, to use the expression "mystic drama" to describe the chöd practice. Although I don't necessarily support his interpretation of the chöd practice as a whole, I feel this description is appropriate.

8 *mKha' 'gro* literally means "skygoer." It is interesting to observe that in most cases the deity is female, though there are cases, like the chöd within the *Ninefold Preliminary Practices* of the *Experiential Transmission of Zhang Zhung*—discussed below—where the consciousness that is expelled directly from the heart outward becomes a male deity. See David Germano, trans., *The Experiential Transmission of Drugyelwa Yungdrung*, Part 1 (Charlottesville, VA: Ligmincha Institute, 1994), 11. Tenzin Wangyal Rinpoche explained that a reason one transforms into a female deity is that one is returning to the source, the womb. Teaching on the chöd practice, Charlottesville, April 1996. See also the translation of *Laughter of the Skygoers* in appendix 1 and my brief discussion in the epilogue.

9 Most texts agree on the description of the four guests: the buddhas and bodhisattvas, the protectors, the eight classes of beings, and the beings of the six realms. Harding states that "Machik counts five distinct parties at this point: (1) the lamas, yidams, ḍākinīs and dharma protectors; (2) karmic creditors; (3) beings of the six realms; (4) good local spirits; and (5) terrifying, hostile gods and demons [or maybe it should be gods-demons]." Sarah Harding, trans. and ed., *Machik's Complete Explanation: Clarifying the Meaning of Chöd* (Ithaca, NY: Snow Lion Publications, 2003), 53. What is important is that all sentient beings are included in those categories. Mumford, in describing the chöd rite performed in Gyamsudo, reports that the eight classes of beings are called "uninvited guests (*'bod ma rung k'i mgron*)," stressing the theme that "no one may be excluded" from this feast. Mumford, *Himalayan Dialogue*, 207.

10 Mumford in *Himalayan Dialogue* mentions the red offering/feast several times, always relating it to an actual animal sacrifice. In teaching the chöd practice, Yongdzin Tenzin Namdak has described the white offerings as a more vegetarian dish and the red one as for the meat-eaters. It depends on what different beings desire.

Dan Martin says that the linkage between sky burial and chöd suggests that the latter "may be (at least in part) understood as a symbolic extension of, or possibly a psychological adaptation to, the cultural fact of corpse dismemberment." "On the Cultural Ecology of Sky Burial on the Himalayan Plateau," *East and West* (Rome) 46 (1996): 13. Heather Stoddard reverses the direction of causality and suggests that it was chöd that influenced the Tibetans to shift their funeral practices from tomb burial to sky burial. "Eat It Up or Throw It to the Dogs? Dge 'Dun chos 'phel (1903–1951), Ma cig lab sgron (1055–1153) and Pha dam pa sangs rgyas (d. 1117): A Ramble through the Burial Grounds of Ordinary and 'Holy' Beings in Tibet," paper presented at IATS XI, Bonn, Germany, 2006. She also presented some parts of this paper in her talk at the Bön conference in Shenten Dargye Ling, France, June 2008. I am very grateful to Heather for sharing this material before publication. Unfortunately, as I also mention in the epilogue, there is not much information available on the relationship between sky burial and chöd, and on which of them came first. Martin observes: "a perceived connection between the two practices made them co-dependent (in some degree) within the culture as a whole." Martin, "On the Cultural Ecology of Sky Burial on the Himalayan Plateau," 15. Harding, cites Madrong, who states that sky burial became popular in Tibet after the mid-eleventh century and suggests that it was inspired by the chöd and Zhi byed traditions. Harding, *Machik's Complete Explanation*, 49 and 293, n. 67.

11 Mumford, *Himalayan Dialogue*, 207.

12 David Snellgrove, *The Nine Ways of Bon* (London: Oxford University Press, 1967), 183.

13 G. Roerich, trans., *The Blue Annals*, by Go Lotsawa Zhonupal (Delhi: Motilal Banarsidas, 1995), 997. The accounts are on pp. 980–1005. Yeshe Dorje Rinpoche was also known to use chöd to bring or stop rain, according to community needs. Being the weatherman for His Holiness the Dalai Lama, he was asked to stop rain during important religious ceremonies, and for example, to bring rain during droughts.

14 There are two curricula that a monk can follow in these monasteries. The majority follow the dialectic curriculum (*mtshan nyid*), which emphasizes scholarly understanding and debate; a small group follows a meditation curriculum (*sgrub grwa*). Only those following the latter perform chöd. However, I have seen nuns performing chöd in groups in monasteries in Tibet.

15 A very well-known scholar told me he considered chöd a funky practice.

16 Jerome Edou, *Machig Labdrön and the Foundations of Chöd* (Ithaca, NY: Snow Lion Publications, 1996), 8.

17 Janet Gyatso, "The Development of the *Gcod* Tradition," in *Soundings in Tibetan Civilization*, ed. Barbara Aziz and Matthew Kapstein, 320–41 (Delhi: Manohar, 1985).

18 Carol Diane Savvas: "A Study of the Profound Path of *Gcod*: The Mahāyāna Buddhist Meditation Tradition of Tibet's Great Woman Saint Machig Labdron" (PhD diss., University of Wisconsin, 1990). Other references include Giuseppe Tucci, *The Religions of Tibet* (Delhi: Allied Publishers, 1980); Giacomella Orofino, *Contributo allo studio dell' insegnamento di Ma gcig Lab sgron* (Naples: Instituto Universitario Orientale, 1987), and "The Great Wisdom Mother and the Gcod Tradition," in *Tantra in Practice*, ed. D. G. White, 398–416 (Princeton: Princeton University Press, 2000); and R. A. Stein, *Tibetan Civilization* (London: Faber and Faber, 1972).

19 Edou, *Machig Labdrön and the Foundations of Chöd*, 177.

20 Harding, *Machik's Complete Explanation*; Kyabje Zong Rinpoche, *Chöd in the*

Ganden Tradition: The Oral Instructions of Kyabje Zong Rinpoche, ed. David Molk (Ithaca, NY: Snow Lion Publications, 2006); Tsultrim Allione, *Feeding Your Demons* (New York: Little, Brown and Co., 2008).

21 Edou acknowledges a Bön tradition of chöd, but states "that it will not be treated in detail in the present study." Edou, *Machig Labdrön and the Foundations of Chöd*, 175. Namkhai Norbu too acknowledges such a tradition and says that it "has not yet been the object of study." N. Norbu, *Drung, Deu, and Bön: Narrations, Symbolic Languages, and the Bön Tradition in Ancient Tibet* (Dharamsala: Library of Tibetan Works and Archives, 1995), 257. Harding also mentions the Bön chöd, its relation to the mu (*dmu*) lineage, and possible similarities with the *gto* ritual. Harding, *Machik's Complete Explanation*, 47, 262, and 307, respectively. She adds in a footnote that sometimes references to Bön might actually be to "the 'so-called Bön po'" that probably indicated a common wandering shaman who performs rituals not clearly rooted in either Bön or Buddhist doctrine (306–7, n. 19).

22 Many of the scholars that have written on this topic seem to have been drawn to the practice first. In the last two decades, chöd has been practiced in many dharma centers such as Namkhai Norbu Rinpoche's Dzogchen Community and Tenzin Wangyal Rinpoche's Ligmincha Institute, among others.

23 Gyatso, "The Development of the *Gcod* Tradition," 340.

24 In "The Development of the *Gcod* Tradition," 340, Gyatso lists the following Bön chöd texts: Tashi Dorje, ed., *Zab lam mkha' 'gro gang ba'i gcod kyi gdams pa* (New Thobgyal: Tibetan Bonpo Monastic Centre, 1973), from the oral transmission received by Tulku Tronyan Gyaltsen (*sPrul sku khro gnyan rgyal mtshan*), from the fourteenth century; Gelong Sonam Gyaltsen, ed., *Mkha' 'gro gsan gcod yid bzin nor bu'i dmigs pa'i skor rnams cha tshan* (Dolanji: Tibetan Bonpo Monastic Centre, 1974), from the vision of Kyantrul Namkha Gyaltsen (*Skyan sprul nam mkha' rgyal mtshan*) of the teachings of Tronyan Gyaltsen; Tashi Dorji, ed., *Mkha' 'gro gsan gcod kyi lag len skor* (Dolanji: Tibetan Bonpo Monastic Centre, 1974), also from Kyantrul Namkha Gyaltsen's vision of the teachings of Tronyan Gyaltsen; Tshultrim Tashi, ed., *Zab lam gnad kyi gdams pa drug mu gcod chen gyi gsun pod* (New Thobgyal: Tibetan Bonpo Monastic Centre, 1973), from the vision of Shense Lhaje (*Gshen gsas lha rje*, flourished before 1310) of Tongyun Thuchen (*Ston rgyun mthu chen*); Tshering Wangyal, ed., *Yum chen kye ma 'od mtsho'i zab gsang gcod kyi gdams pa las phran dang bcas pa'i gsung pod* (Dolanji: Tibetan Bonpo Monastic Centre, 1974), the revelations of Khandro Dechen Wangmo (*Mkha' 'gro bde chen dbang mo*, b. 1868); and Nyagter Sangngag Lingpa (*Nyag gter gsan sngags glin pa*), *Zab mo gcod kyi gdams nag yum chen thugs rje sgrol ma*, ed. Patshang Lama Sonam Gyaltsen (New Thobgyal: Tibetan Bonpo Monastic Centre, 1973).

25 Gyatso, "The Development of the *Gcod* Tradition," 340.

26 Norbu, *Drung, Deu, and Bön*, 257; Samten Karmay, *A Catalogue of Bonpo Publications* (Tokyo: The Toyo Bunko, 1977), 89–93. These chöd texts are also included in Gyatso's list given above. See appendix 3 for more information on these texts.

27 Edou, *Machig Labdrön and the Foundations of Chöd*, 94. On pp. 224–25 of his bibliography, he adds some detail to the four texts he mentions from Gyatso's list, which I have compiled in appendix 3 to form an annotated bibliography of chöd texts in the Bön tradition.

28 Ibid., 9.

29 John Myrdhin Reynolds, *The Practice of Chod in the Bon Tradition* (San Diego: Vidyadhara Publications, 1996), 7. David Germano translated *The Experiential Transmission of Drugyelwa Yungdrung* into English. This text is the ngondro, which contains nine practices, one of which is chöd. This is a very brief chöd, not the *Laughter of the Skygoers*.

30 Reynolds does not mention any texts from the New Bön tradition that were not also included in Gyatso's account.

31 Reynolds, *The Practice of Chod in the Bon Tradition*, 7.

32 Annette Jones, "Transgressive Compassion: The Role of Fear, Horror, and the Threat of Death in Ultimate Transformation" (PhD diss., Rice University, 1998). In her dissertation, Jones translates the chöd text *Precious Garland of Severance Instructions* (*gCod gdams rin chen phreng ba*) by Drung mu ha ra, which is included in the collection of chöd texts *Zab lam gnad kyi dgams pa drug mu gcod chen gyi gsun pod*, mentioned above in the texts Gyatso lists.

33 Donatella Rossi, "A Preliminary Survey of the mKha' 'gro gsang gcod Teachings of Bon" (paper presented at IATS XI, Bonn, Germany, August 2006).

34 Dan Martin, *Mandala Cosmogony: Human Body Good Thought and the Revelation of the Secret Mother Tantras of Bon* (Wiesbaden: Harrassowitz Verlag, 1994); and "The Emergence of Bon and the Tibetan Polemical Tradition" (PhD diss., Indiana University, 1991); Reynolds, *The Practice of Chod in the Bon Tradition*; *Yungdrung Bon, The Eternal Tradition: The Ancient Pre-Buddhist Religion of Central Asia and Tibet: Its History, Teachings, and Literature* (Freehold, NJ: Bonpo Translation Project, 1991); *The Mother Tantra from the Bon Tradition* (San Diego: Bonpo Translation Project/Bonpo Research Foundation, 1993—work in progress); *The Threefold Practice of the Primordial State of the Mother Tantra* (San Diego: Vidyadhara Publications, 1996); *The Mandala of the Sun* (San Diego: Bonpo Translation Project, 1996—work in progress). I thank him for allowing me to use his works-in-progress.

35 Edou utilizes this term for the Tibetan chöd (*bod gcod*) to distinguish it from the Indian chöd, which comes from the precepts taught by Āryadeva and

Padampa Sangye, among others, and emphasizes the sūtra tradition. Edou, *Machig Labdrön and the Foundations of Chöd*, 7 and 31–38.

36　Ibid., 6. I added the Tibetan, which Edou has in a footnote on p. 176.

37　Ibid., 6–7.

38　Below I will discuss how contentious is the category of shamanism even today.

39　Edou, *Machig Labdrön and the Foundations of Chöd*, 9. The *Jātaka* stories recount the previous lives of the Buddha, stressing the bodhisattvic altruistic ideal. Among the works that Edou criticizes for their shamanic interpretations of chöd, he mentions C. Van Tuyl, "Mi-la-ras-pa and the gCod Ritual," *Tibet Journal* 4 (1979); Mircea Eliade, *Shamanism: Archaic Techniques of Ecstasy*, Bollingen Foundation Series 76 (New York: Bollingen, 1964); Evans-Wentz, *Tibetan Yoga and Secret Doctrines*; E. Bleichsteiner, *L'église jaune* (Paris: Payot, 1950), first published as *Die gelbe Kirche* (Vienna, 1937); and A. David-Neel, *Magic and Mystery in Tibet* (New York: HarperCollins, 1993), first published as *Parmi les mystiques et les magiciens du Tibet* (Paris: Libraire Plon, 1929). The relationship of chöd to the *Jātaka* tales is beyond the scope of the present study, although I will briefly mention it in the epilogue.

40　Yongdzin Tenzin Namdak recommends that practitioners get familiar with chöd by practicing first for three years in peaceful places such as a shrine room. This serves as a preparation before actually going to the frightening places and practicing chöd there.Yongdzin Tenzin Namdak, personal communication, Kathmandu, June 1997.

41　Norbu, *The Crystal and the Way of Light*, 47–49.

42　Geoffrey Samuel, *Civilized Shamans: Buddhism in Tibetan Societies* (Washington: Smithsonian Institution Press, 1993), 7–23.

43　Ibid., 8. For more discussion on his usage of the concept of "shamanic," see G. Samuel, *Mind, Body, and Culture: Anthropology and the Biological Interface* (New York: Cambridge University Press, 1990).

44　Samuel, *Civilized Shamans*, 8. He also directs the reader to G. Samuel, "The Body in Buddhist and Hindu Tantra: Some Notes," *Religion* 19 (1989): 197–210.

45　George Dreyfus, *The Sound of Two Hands Clapping: The Education of a Tibetan Buddhist Monk* (Berkeley: University of California Press, 2003), 336–37, n. 18. Thanks to Michele Sorensen for directing me to this discussion.

46　Ibid., 336.

47　Per Kvaerne, "Bon and the Problem of Shamanism" (paper presented at the International Conference on Bon, Shenten Dargye Ling, France, June 22–25, 2008). I appreciate Dr. Kvaerne's permission to use his presentation before its publication. Kvaerne based his interpretation on the work of another distinguished Scandinavian scholar, anthropologist Ake Hulkranz.

48 Dimitri Ermakov, *Bo and Bon: Ancient Shamanic Traditions of Siberia and Tibet and Their Relation to the Teachings of a Central Asian Buddhism* (Kathmandu: Vajra Publications, 2008), lii.

49 Samuel, *Civilized Shamans*, 8.

50 Geoffrey Samuel, *Tantric Revisionings* (New Delhi: Motilal Banarsidas and Ashgate, 2005); and *The Origins of Yoga and Tantra: Indic Religions to the Thirteenth Century* (London: Cambridge University Press, 2008).

51 Samuel, *Civilized Shamans*, 6.

52 G. Samuel, "Shamanism, Bon, and Tibetan Religion," in *Tantric Revisionings* (New Delhi: Motilal Banarsidas and Ashgate), 132.

53 Harding, *Machik's Complete Explanation*, 43.

54 Sarah Harding, following Khenpo Tsultrim Gyamtso Rinpoche, points out that *lha 'dre*, which is the term translated here as "gods and demons" could actually be better conceived as one word, "god-demons" since "when these god-demons are in a positive mood, they will help you, then they are beneficial. But when they are hurt, they will harm you in turn." Ibid., 39.

55 Namkhai Norbu, *The Dzogchen Ritual Practices*, ed. and trans. Brian Beresford (London: Kailash Editions, 1991), 199.

56 Some chöd texts actually include a particular dance. The *Chöd of the Secret Skygoers*, for example, has a dance that very few people still know how to do. One person who does is Lama Tashi from Dolpo, and Ligmincha Institute is in the process of recording him performing the dance as part of an archive that soon may take a form that can be shared.

57 See Gyatso, "The Development of the *Gcod* Tradition," 324; Edou, *Machig Labdrön and the Foundations of Chöd*, 39; Savvas, "A Study of the Profound Path of *Gcod*," 1–3; and G. Roerich, *Blue Annals*, 980–83.

58 Edou, *Machig Labdrön and the Foundations of Chöd*, 39.

59 Jamgön Kontrul, "The Profound Perfection of Insight Practice of Severing Demons" (*bDud kyi gcod yul sher phyin zab mo'i spyod*), Compendium, 420, quoted in Edou, *Machig Labdrön and the Foundations of Chöd*, 39.

60 Edou shows this equivalence of terminology in *Machig Labdrön and the Foundations of Chöd*, 213.

61 C. Savvas, "A Study of the Profound Path of *Gcod*," 1.

62 Ven. Geshe Champa Lodro Rinpoche, "Public Discourse on the gCod Practice," talk presented in Switzerland, 1990, quoted in Savvas, "A Study of the Profound Path of *Gcod*," 1.

63 *The Eight Extraordinary Chapters*, in *gDams Ngag mDzod*, ed. Kongtrul Lodro Thaye (*Kong sprul blo gros mtha 'yas*) and newly edited by Dingo Chhentse Rinpoche, 18 vols. (Paro, Bhutan: Lama Ngodrup and Sherap Drimey), vol. 14, p. 153, quoted in Savvas, "A Study of the Profound Path of *Gcod*," 2.

64 Edou, *Machig Labdrön and the Foundations of Chöd*, 10.

65 Ibid.

66 Ibid. Edou does not define his use of the term "shamanism," although he mentions Eliade, Bleichsteiner, and Van Tuyl in this context.

67 Huber, "Putting the *gnas* Back into the *gnas-skor*: Rethinking Tibetan Buddhist Pilgrimage Practice," *Tibet Journal* 19 (1994): 24. The terms "emic" and "etic" were coined by the linguistic anthropologist Kenneth Pike to refer to the two perspectives, insider and outsider, that can be used to study a given society. The emic is the insider's perspective, which Pike defines as the intrinsic cultural distinctions that are meaningful to the members of a given society. Kenneth L. Pike, *Language in Relation to a Unified Theory of the Structure of Human Behavior*, 2nd. ed. (The Hague: Mouton, 1967).

68 Savvas, "A Study of the Profound Path of *Gcod*," ix. Conze expresses this belief in *Buddhist Thought in India* (London: Allen and Unwin, 1962), 270.

69 Edou, *Machig Labdrön and the Foundations of Chöd*, 7. It does seem that chöd practitioners preferred this type of lifestyle and practiced in cemeteries and charnel grounds in order to inspire fear that then can be severed. I do, however, acknowledge that chöd is also practiced, in many cases, in a monastic environment. My understanding is that, in the majority of cases, performing chöd in such peaceful environments is regarded as "practice" so that they can later go to fearful places and actually perform chöd there.

70 Thanks to Michelle Sorensen who made this point about the practice of chöd in Nyingma monasteries, in conversation at the IATS XI conference, Bonn, August 2006. Tucci mentions a monastic (i.e., clerical) chöd tradition that had its chief monastery in Dingri, Tibet, but the mainstream of this practice is not found in monasteries. Tucci, *The Religions of Tibet*, 87. Other scholars, for example, Michelle Sorensen, have challenged the claim that chöd is not a monastic practice. See M. Sorensen, "The Body Extraordinary: Lus kyil praxis and gCod" (paper presented at IATS XI, Bonn, Germany, 2006), a paper based on her fieldwork observations.

71 I suggest that this topic might deserve an anthropological rather than a textual study. The question to investigate is whether the chöpas who practice in fearful places maintain the same philosophical view as those who practice in a monastic setting and have never practiced in fearful locations.

72 Samuel, *Civilized Shamans*, 8. In a footnote, he mentions that a few scholars have written about the connection between yoga and shamanism: Barbara Aziz, "Reincarnation Reconsidered: Or the Reincarnate Lama as Shaman," in *Spirit Possession in the Nepal Himalayas*, ed. John T. Hitchcock and Rex L. Jones (Warminster: Aris and Phillips), 343–60; Mircea Eliade, *Yoga: Immortality and Freedom* (New York: Pantheon, 1958); and *Shamanism*; and Wil-

liam Stablein, "The Mahākālatantra: A Theory of Ritual Blessings and Tantric Medicine" (PhD diss., Columbia University, 1976).

73 Samuel, *Civilized Shamans*, 5–10.

74 Ibid., 8.

75 Harding, *Machik's Complete Explanation*, 47.

76 Norbu, *The Dzogchen Ritual Practices*, 199.

77 Ibid., 200.

78 Edou, *Machig Labdrön and the Foundations of Chöd*, 10.

79 Brad Leithauser, *The Norton Book of Ghost Stories* (New York: W. W. Norton and Company, 1994), 14 – 15. Although Leithauser's comment is about ghost stories, not chöd, I find his remark appropriate to illustrate this point.

80 Harding, *Machik's Complete Explanation*, 46.

81 Gyatso, "The Development of the *Gcod* Tradition," 322–23.

82 Note that the "outrageous" lifestyle of chöpas can also be considered a part of tantra. For example, some scholars, especially those who study Hinduism, have talked about a "left" and "right" tantra.

83 Mumford, *Himalayan Dialogue*, 163. Mumford cites Eliade, *Shamanism*, and Joan Halifax, *Shamanic Voices* (New York: E. P. Dutton, 1979), who mention this kind of dismemberment as a characteristic of shamanic initiations throughout inner Asia.

84 Harding, *Machik's Complete Explanation*, 46.

85 Mumford, *Himalayan Dialogue*, 161.

86 Gyatso, "The Development of the *Gcod* Tradition," 322. Gyatso cites R. A. Stein, *Tibetan Civilization*, trans. J. E. Stapleton Driver (Stanford: Stanford University Press, 1972), 211ff.

87 Reynolds, *The Practice of Chod in the Bon Tradition*, 3.

88 Harding, *Machik's Complete Explanation*, 47. However, her wording may suggest some of the controversy about the relationship of Buddhism to Bön and vice versa that will be discussed in the next chapter.

89 See Snellgrove, *The Nine Ways of Bon*, 9–13. Snellgrove claims that all Tibetan Buddhist sects include rituals in their practices that can be said to have a shamanic origin, or be part of the Bön Causal Vehicles (*rgyu'i bon*)—such as fumigation rituals (*sang mchod*), divination (*mo*), and putting up prayer flags (*rlung rta*)—although they do not categorize them as such.

Chöd in the Bön Religion

90 S. Karmay, "A General Introduction to the History and Doctrines of Bon," in *Memoirs of the Research Department of the Toyo Bunko* 33: 171–218.

91 Martin, *Mandala Cosmogony*, 6. For a study of the polemical tradition in

greater detail, see also Martin, "The Emergence of Bon and the Tibetan Polemical Tradition."

92 Martin, "The Emergence of Bon and the Tibetan Polemical Tradition," 3.

93 Martin, *Mandala Cosmogony*, 5.

94 Per Kvaerne, *The Bon Religion of Tibet: The Iconography of a Living Tradition* (Boston: Shambhala Publications, 1996), 10. See also Dan Martin, *Unearthing Bon Treasures* (Leiden: Brill, 2001), 30–39. His Holiness the Fourteenth Dalai Lama states: "The Bon tradition, which had existed in Tibet before the arrival of Buddhism, also came to possess a complete set of the Buddha's teachings." The Dalai Lama, *A Flash of Lightning in the Dark of Night: A Guide to the Bodhisattva's Way of Life* (Boston: Shambhala Publications, 1994), 7.

95 See P. Kvaerne, "Aspects of the Origin of the Buddhist Tradition in Tibet," *Numen* 19 (1972): 22–40.

96 Kvaerne, *The Bon Religion of Tibet*, 10. See also Martin, "The Emergence of Bon and the Tibetan Polemical Tradition," and *Mandala Cosmogony;* and D. Snellgrove, *The Nine Ways of Bon*, and *Indo-Tibetan Buddhism: Indian Buddhists and Their Tibetan Successors* (London: Serindia Publications, 1987).

97 Martin, "The Emergence of Bon and the Tibetan Polemical Tradition," 86.

98 David L. Snellgrove and Hugh E. Richardson, *A Cultural History of Tibet* (Boulder: Prajna Press, 1980), 175.

99 The Tibetan Government in exile in Dharamsala has had Bön representatives as part of their Assembly since the early 1970s (Rinchen Dharlo, former representative of His Holiness the Dalai Lama to the Americas, personal communication, August 1998). Also, the 1991 Kalachakra teachings and initiation by His Holiness the Dalai Lama in New York City marked quite a historical event when leading teachers from all five traditions gave teachings on the nature of mind from their own perspectives. Yongdzin Tenzin Namdak gave those teachings from the Bön tradition's point of view.

100 Kvaerne, *The Bon Religion of Tibet*, 11.

101 Vairocana, *Authenticity* (*Gtan tshigs Gal mdo rig pa's tshad ma*), 128.4, quoted in Anne C. Klein and Geshe Tenzin Wangyal Rinpoche, *Unbounded Wholeness: Dzogchen, Bon, and the Logic of the Nonconceptual* (Oxford: Oxford University Press, 2006), 198.

102 Reynolds, *Yungdrung Bon, The Eternal Tradition*, 7.

103 Snellgrove, *The Nine Ways of Bon*, 1.

104 David Germano, *Dzogchen Mini-Encyclopaedia* (Charlottesville: University of Virginia, 1994), 660. Change of Tibetan capitalization is mine.

105 Martin, *Mandala Cosmogony*, 11.

106 Some consider Olmo Lungring to be the same as the region of Shambhala in Buddhist accounts. In both cases, it has been difficult for scholars to determine

whether this land actually existed on the face of our planet or if it is a mythical land. For a brief discussion on this, see Karmay, "A General Introduction to the History and Doctrines of Bon," 10–15; and Klein and Wangyal, *Unbounded Wholeness*, 171–79.

107 Giacomella Orofino, "The State of the Art in the Study of the Zhang zhung Language," *Annali* 50, fasc. 1 (Italy: Istituto Universitaro Orientale, 1990), 83. I will use "Zhang Zhung"—both words beginning with a capital "Z" for the place and "Zhang zhung" for the language.

108 For more information on the Zhang zhung language, see E. Haar, *The Zhang-Zhung Language: A Grammar and Dictionary of the Unexplored Language of the Tibetan Bonpos*, Acta Jutlantica 40 (Kobenhavn: University of Aarhus, 1968). Haar's work is based on Yongdzin Tenzin Namdak, *Dictionary of the Zhang zhung Language* (n.p., n.d.).

109 Martin, "The Emergence of Bon and the Tibetan Polemical Tradition," 92. The lack of hyphenation in Tibetan phonetic is mine.

110 Tonpa Shenrab is said to have been born in the year 16,016 BCE and to have died in 7,816 BCE, which would mean he lived over eight thousand years. See P. Kvaerne, "A Chronological Table of the Bon po: The *Bstan rcis* of Ñi ma bstan 'jin," *Acta Orientalia* 33 (1971): 205–82. Martin adds that, "The original Tibetan work on which this article is based was composed by Nyi-ma-bstan-'dzin in 1842." Martin, *Unearthing Bon Treasures*, 366. Martin also mentions that a fourteenth-century source dates Tonpa Shenrab from 4,074 through 974 BCE. Martin, *Unearthing Bon Treasures*, 10, n. 1.

111 *'Chi med*, meaning "no death" or "immortal," is "an epithet of Buddha." Chandra Das, *Tibetan-English Dictionary*, compact ed. (Delhi: Book Faith India, 1992), 444.

112 This is one way in which Tenzin Wangyal Rinpoche translated it (personal communication, November 1998); it could also be rendered as "Secret Gathering."

113 Yongdzin Tenzin Namdak explained Lhabu Dampa Karpo's purity as being that of a crystal, and referred to him as "Crystal Boy." Oral teachings, Mexico, June 1998.

114 Yongdzin Tenzin Namdak, oral teachings, Mexico, June 1998. Martin points out that Tonpa Shenrab's medium-length biography in two volumes (*Gzer mig*) and his long biography in twelve volumes (*Gzi rjid*) not only have a certain similarity to Buddha Shākyamuni's and Guru Rinpoche's lives, but also to the epics of Gesar and the Indian Rāmāyana. Martin, *Unearthing Bon Treasures*, 33. Martin also suggests that "the Bon parallels may actually precede the versions of the Gesar epic that have come down to us." Martin, *Unearthing Bon Treasures*, 33, n. 11.

115 Reynolds, *The Threefold Practice of the Primordial State of the Mother Tantra*, 1.
116 Ibid.
117 Martin, *Mandala Cosmogony*, 9. He refers to a "privately circulated draft" in which Beckwith describes this relationship between the *bwn* and *dharma* while analyzing a famous Iranian cosmological work, *Bundahisn*, in which the term *bwn* means "construct," which is another meaning of *dharma* or *chos*.
118 Ibid. Change of capitalization and lack of hyphenation in the Tibetan transliteration is mine.
119 Stoddard, "Eat It Up or Throw It to the Dogs?"
120 Shardza Tashi Gyaltsen, *The Treasury of Good Sayings* (*Legs bshad mdzod*), in Samten Karmay, ed. and trans., *The Treasury of Good Sayings: A Tibetan History of Bon* (London: Oxford University Press, 1972), quoted in Klein and Wangyal, *Unbounded Wholeness*, 199.
121 Klein and Wangyal, *Unbounded Wholeness*, 199.
122 The Nine Ways will be discussed just below. As for a list of the Five Doors, also called the Four Doors and the Treasure, see Reynolds, *Yungdrung Bon*, 7, and p. 6 of his appendix.
123 Snellgrove, *Nine Ways of Bon*. Snellgrove worked with Yongdzin Tenzin Namdak, Geshe Samten Karmay, and Geshe Sangye Tenzin Jongdong (who today is His Holiness Lungtok Tenpai Nyima, the holder of the throne of Menri Monastery), making this the first Euro-American translation of a Bön teaching. It is also important to note that the system of Nine Vehicles in the Buddhist Nyingma tradition is different from the Nine Ways in Bön; they are similar only in the number of vehicles into which they divide the teachings. Actually there are three different versions of the Nine Ways within the Bön tradition, the most popular one—the one that Snellgrove translated—is according to the Southern treasure (*lho gter*), or the rediscovery found in the south of the country. There is also a version according to the Northern treasure (*byang gter*) and another according to the Central treasure (*dbus gter*). See Karmay, "A General Introduction to the History and Doctrines of Bon," 178–79; Katsumi Mimaki, "A Fourteenth-Century Bon Po Doxography," in *Bon Sgo Gsal Byed: Two Tibetan Manuscripts in Facsimile Edition of a Fourteenth-Century Encyclopedia of Bon Po Doxography* (Tokyo: Centre for East Asian Cultural Studies for Unesco, Toyo Bunko, 1997); K. Mimaki, "The *Bon sgo byed* by Tre ston rgyal mtshan dpal–A Preliminary Report toward a Critical Edition," in *Proceedings of the 6th Seminar of the International Association of Tibetan Studies, Fagernes 1992*, Vol. 2, ed. P. Kvaerne, 570–79 (Oslo: The Institute for Comparative Research in Human Culture, 1994). For a listing of the vehicles in all three treasures, see Reynolds, *Yungdrung Bon*, 7 and p. 5 of his appendix.
    Shardza Rinpoche did a study of the three nine-way classifications in *Lung*

rig rin po che'i mdzod blo gsal snying gi nor. See Karmay, *A Catalogue of Bönpo Publications,* 171–72. The Nine Ways system, together with the Five Doors, are the base of what is called Yungdrung Bön (*g.Yung drung bon*), which is the old Bön system that Yongdzin Tenzin Namdak follows and which will be briefly discussed below.

124 Yongdzin Tenzin Namdak, oral communication, Sunrise Springs, New Mexico, August 1998, and on other occasions.

125 R. A. Stein, *La Cilvilisation Tibétaine,* quoted in P. Kvaerne, "The Bön Religion of Tibet: A Survey of Research," in *The Buddhist Forum,* Vol. 3, ed. T. Skorupski and U. Pagel (London: School of Oriental and African Studies, 1994), 134; Giuseppe Tucci, *The Religions of Tibet.*

126 Klein and Wangyal state: "Dranpa Namkha [*Dran pa rnam kha'*] and Vairocana are among the main persons who integrated old and new Bon for the first time." Klein and Wangyal, *Unbounded Wholeness,* 179. However, they add that it was not practiced until the seventeenth century, after the impulse of the four masters also known as "the four tulkus," who are Sangye Lingpa (*Sangs rgyas gling pa,* b.1705), Loden Nyingpo (*Blo ldan snying po,* b. 1360), Kundrol Drakpa (*Kun grol grags pa,* b. 1700), and Mishik Dorje (*Mi shig rdo rje,* b. 1650). They also refer the reader to Karmay's translation of Shardza's *The Treasury of Good Sayings.*

127 In particular there is discussion about the origin of the Dzogchen teachings, both in Bön and Buddhism. Karmay talks of the three Dzogchen systems (*A rdzogs snyan gsum*) within the Bön tradition, dating the earliest, the *Zhang zhung snyan rgyud,* to the eighth century, and the other two, *A khrid* and *Rdzogs chen,* to the eleventh century—for the latter, 1088 was the date of rediscovery. See Karmay, "A General Introduction to the History and Doctrines of Bon," 215. Namkhai Norbu also discusses the origin of the Dzogchen teachings, claiming that these teachings came from Tazig and were propounded by the Buddha Shenrab Miwo. Namkhai Norbu, *The Necklace of gZi: A Cultural History of Tibet* (Dharamsala, India: Narthang Publications, 1981), 15–18.

128 As mentioned above, the Nyingma school also has a system of Nine Ways or Nine Vehicles. In fact their system is similar to that of the Bönpo Central Treasure. See Mimaki, "A Fourteenth-Century Bon Po Doxography."

129 I would like to mention here a conversation I had with Samdong Rinpoche, a Gelug Lama and head of the kashag (*bka' shag*), the Tibetan Parliament in exile. He mentioned how many Bön practices have been incorporated by Tibetan Buddhism and are now part of the culture, such as displaying prayer flags, the smoke ritual (*sangs mchod*), and so forth. Buenos Aires, 1998. This seems to be a view shared by most Tibetan Buddhists. What I would like to point out here is that although Tibetan Buddhists use these rituals within their religion,

they tend to talk about them as part of their culture rather than their religion. This is also reflected in their doxographies, where we do not find the practices that are part of the causal vehicles. This is also the case with Tibetan medicine, which has an ambiguous place within Tibetan Buddhism: it is included in tantric practice but is also a category in itself and can be practiced with or without religion. However, by leaving these practices as part of Tibetan culture but not part of Tibetan religion, Tibetans also leave it out of their philosophy. This might explain why we see a dichotomy between the chöpa's lifestyle and his supposed adherence to philosophical beliefs.

130 See Snellgrove, *The Nine Ways of Bon*, and Kvaerne, "The Bon Religion of Tibet." In the latter article, Kvaerne also explains Euro-American scholars' understanding of the Bön religion and its development, particularly around the issue of pre- and post-Buddhist Bön, which this book will not discuss.

131 Kvaerne, "The Bon Religion of Tibet," 135.

132 It is also important to bear in mind, as David Germano clarifies, that "Bön was also a rubric right into the twentieth century for 'shamanic' type practitioners who had little interest or concern with such sophisticated Bön movements [like Yungdrung Bön]." D. Germano, electronic correspondence, August 1998.

133 These four parallel the four kinds of enlightened activities: peaceful (*zhi*), developing (*rgyas*), conquering (*dbang*), and wrathful (*drag*). English preface, Tulku Tronyan Gyaltsen, *Zab lam mkha' 'gro gsan ba'i gcod kyi gdams pa.* Change of capital letter in Tibetan titles and italics are mine. He adds in parenthesis, in the preface written in 1973, that the *A dkar zhi gcod* "has still not been located in India or Nepal." In 1986 though, Yongdzin Tenzin Namdak Rinpoche visited Tibet and obtained a copy of it which was handwritten by, and belonged to, the one who succeeded him as Lopon in Menri Monastery (*sMan ri*) , who by then had already passed away. It is not yet published.

134 See Karmay, "A General Introduction to the History and Doctrines of Bon," 215.

135 English preface, Shense Lhaje, *Zab lam gnad kyi gdams pa drug mu gcod chen gyi gsu pod.* Italics, noncapitalized syllables, and the lack of hyphenation in the Tibetan transliteration is mine. Shense Lhaje was actually called Drungmu Hara (*Drung mu hara*), a Zhang zhung name that is translated into Tibetan as Yungdrung Yeshe (*g.Yung drung ye shes*).

136 Some sādhanas, for example, this one, include dancing together with the liturgy. Only one lama still knew the dance when I was finishing my MA Thesis. He lived in the northwest Nepali area of Dolpo and has recently transmitted his knowledge to another lama in his lineage, Geshe Lama Tashi Gyaltsen. As mentioned earlier, we have recorded Lama Tashi at Ligmincha Institute, and we hope to make it available soon.

137 English preface, Tulku Tronyan Gyaltsen, *Zab lam mkha' 'gro gsan ba'i gcod kyi gdams pa*. Italics, noncapitalized syllables, and the lack of hyphenation in the Tibetan transliteration is mine.

138 English preface, Nyagter Sangngag Lingpa, *Zab mo gcod kyi gdams nag yum chen thugs rje sgrol ma*. It is important to note that the Yungdrung Bön considers the New Bön as not pure Bön, but a *mélange* of Bön and Buddhism. The rise of the New Bön tradition is probably also the source of much of the confusion which leads to the polemics referred to earlier.

139 Reynolds, *The Threefold Practice of the Primordial State of the Mother Tantra*, 6. As mentioned earlier, chöd is one of the six practices of the path of meditation in the *Secret Mother Tantra*.

140 Shardza Tashi Gyaltsen, *gSang sngags ma rgyud gnyan sa lam 'khyer gyi gcod kyi khrid yig bdud bzhi tshar gcod*, 520–21, which reads as follows: de la spyir gcod la zhi rgyas dbang drag gi gcod chen po bzhi yod de/ gang zhe na/ snang srid zhi bder gnas pa'i phyir/ zhi gcod 'phrul gyi lde mig bstan/ tshe bsod dbang thang rgyas pa'i phyir/ gcod chen ri rgyal lhun po bstan/ dbang chen sde brgyad 'dul ba'i phyir/ gsang gcod yid bzhin nor bu bstan/ gdon chen ar la gtad pa'i phyir/ drag gcod gnam lcags thog mda' bstan/ zhes de dag kun las mchog tu gyur pa ni/ ma rgyud thugs rje nyi ma'i lam drug gi nang tshan kun tu bzang po'i zhal nas gsungs pa'i gnyan sa lam khyer gyi rgyud 'di nyid yin te/ rgyud kyi 'grel pa'ang rgyal gshen chen pos gsungs pa'i phyir.

141 Tshog gyi Dagmo is the protector of the chöd practice. Each of the six methods of the path of meditation—which will be mentioned later—relates to one of the six skygoers who protect each of those practices of the path of meditation. There is also a beautiful thangka (see figure 2) in which the central figure is the main deity of the *Secret Mother Tantra*, Sangchog Gyalpo (*gSang mchog rgyal po*) in union with his consort Chema Wotsho (*Kye ma 'od mtsho*) and is surrounded by these six skygoers. See figure 2: the red skygoer on the lower left side (from the viewer's perspective) is Tshog gyi Dagmo.

142 Yongdzin Tenzin Namdak, personal communication, Kathmandu, June 1997. Also, as mentioned earlier, Edou quotes Yongdzin Tenzin Namdak as saying that the Bön traditions of chöd follow the highest tantras [and dzogchen].

143 Buddhist chöd texts have similar, although not identical, categories.

144 Tsultrim Allione, "Feeding Your Demons," *Tricycle*, Summer 2008. Adapted from her book of the same name, *Feeding Your Demons* (New York: Little, Brown, and Company, 2008).

145 See Norbu, *Dzogchen Ritual Practices*, 198–200.

146 Machig Labdrön, *Namshä Chenmo*, 109–110, quoted in Savvas, "A Study of the Profound Path of gCod," 83.

147 The five "classical" afflictions that distract one from one's natural state are

ignorance (*ma rig pa*), attachment or desire (*'dod chags*), anger (*zhe sdang*), pride (*nga rgyal*), and jealousy (*phrag tog*), where the first three are the chief ones. Fear and hope are considered to be within, and provide fuel for, each of the afflictions.

148 In the section on chöd, the *Blue Annals* report: "even in the Prajnaparamita mention was made of practices which imitated those of the Tantras . . . [chöd] agrees with the standpoint of the Hevajra-Tantra." Roerich, *Blue Annals*, 980.

149 Karmay, *A Catalogue of Bonpo Publications*, 20. Note that Karmay is referring here to the nine ways as classified in the Southern treasure system.

150 Among the three modes of classifications of the nine vehicles in the Bön tradition, the Central treasure is the most elaborate regarding the classes of tantra. See K. Mimaki, "Doxographie tibétaine et classifications indiennes," in *Actes du colloque franco-japonais de septembre 1991*, ed. Fumimasa Fukui and Gérard Fussman, 126–32 (Paris: École française d'Extrême-Orient, 1994).

151 A thorough explanation of the generation and completion stages are outside the scope of this book, and so I direct the reader to the following: H.H. the Dalai Lama, Tsong-ka-pa, and Jeffrey Hopkins, *Deity Yoga: In Action and Performance Tantra* (Ithaca, NY: Snow Lion Publications, 1981); David Germano, *Dzogchen Mini-Encyclopedia*; Daniel Cozort, *Highest Yoga Tantra* (Ithaca, NY: Snow Lion Publications, 2005); and Jamgön Kongtrul, *Creation and Completion: Essential Points of Tantric Meditation*, 2nd ed., trans. Sarah Harding (Somerville, MA: Wisdom Publications, 2002), among others.

152 Martin, *Mandala Cosmogony*, 32.

153 Norbu, *The Necklace of gZi*, 19.

154 Martin, *Mandala Cosmogony*, 54-55. The modification of capitalized letters and the lack of hyphenation in the Tibetan transliteration is mine. Martin also directs the reader to Karmay, *The Treasury of Good Sayings*, 125-26; and Norbu, *The Necklace of gZi*, 19. As for the *External Mother Tantra*, it was rediscovered by Shenchen Luga (*gShen chen klu dga*), also in the tenth to eleventh centuries.

155 Martin, *Mandala Cosmogony*, 27.

156 Ibid.

157 Reynolds, *The Threefold Practice of the Primordial State of the Mother Tantra*, 7. Martin adds that there is another chronology that "actually dates Lha 'bum *before* the first *rab-'byung* (beginning in 1027 A.D.), but according to Kvaerne (in 'Chronological' no. 97), he was born in 1136 A.D." Martin, *Mandala Cosmogony*, 27. The latter is also the date found in the English preface to the 1985 edition of the *Secret Mother Tantra* text, whereas the preface to the 1971 edition places Guru Nontse in some unspecified time after the texts' burial in the eighth century.

158 Reynolds, *The Threefold Practice of the Primordial State of the Mother Tantra*, 2. It is important to note that when most of the authors quoted in this book refer to the *Mother Tantra*, they are actually referring to the *Secret Mother Tantra*. This will become clear below.

159 Ibid. Italics are mine.

160 Both of these have been utilized as translations of *thig le nyag gcig*. The latter phrase is also the title of a recently published book on Bön Dzogchen logic. See Klein and Wangyal, *Unbounded Wholeness*.

161 Reynolds, *The Threefold Practice of the Primordial State of the Mother Tantra*, 3. Italics, noncapitalized syllables, and the lack of hyphenation in the Tibetan transliteration is mine.

162 Therefore, following Martin, this would agree with the quadruply translated texts that went from "divine language" (*lha'i skad*) to Sanskrit to Tazig to Zhang zhung to Tibetan. Martin, "The Emergence of Bon and the Tibetan Polemical Tradition," 92.

163 Reynolds, *The Threefold Practice of the Primordial State of the Mother Tantra*, 7.

164 Martin, *Mandala Cosmogony*, 28.

165 Reynolds, *The Threefold Practice of the Primordial State of the Mother Tantra*, 7. The lack of hyphenation in the Tibetan transliteration is mine.

166 Yongdzin Tenzin Namdak, personal communication, Houston, June 1996 and reiterated in Kathmandu, June 1997. It is interesting to note that many of the Bön treasures were discovered in this accidental manner after they were hidden because of the persecutions. This differs from the Buddhist tradition where the treasures were discovered by people who were considered to be reincarnations of disciples of Guru Rinpoche, who had hidden those teachings because the people were not ready for them. While the Bön discoverers (*gter ston*) were usually ordinary, and often illiterate people, the Buddhist discoverers were considered great masters that brought forth those teachings when people were ripe for them. In that sense the Buddhist discoveries were predetermined, that is, who was going to discover what text, and when, was foretold by Guru Rinpoche or other great masters or deities (especially skygoers). In contrast, the Bön tradition claims that many of its treasure discoveries were not predetermined but accidental—sometimes even robbers would be the discoverers. However, they too have some treasures that were discovered by great masters or people like Guru Nontse who may be "charismatically" related to the institutors of the lineage. The topic of discovered treasures is very interesting, and the contrast between the accidental (or seemingly accidental) and the predetermined models might bring forth some further information about the similarities and differences between Bön and Buddhism, but is outside the scope of this study.

167 Yongdzin Tenzin Namdak affirms that even though Guru Nontse is often considered to be a teacher and scholar, in actuality he was no scholar. Yongdzin Tenzin Namdak, personal communication, Kathmandu, June 1997.

168 Martin, *Mandala Cosmogony*, 28.

169 Ibid., 29. It is unclear whether the tigresses themselves are the skygoers or if the skygoers are riding on tigresses. The lack of hyphenation in Tibetan transliteration is mine.

170 Martin acknowledges that it is unclear as to "which texts, precisely, were supposed to be 'missing' because they weren't successfully copied [and] because of inconsistency in the attribution of titles to the different commentarial cycles." D. Martin, electronic correspondence, November 1998.

171 This version is just a little longer than an outline; it merely mentions and very succinctly describes, the forty-five wisdom spheres (*ye shes thig le zhe lnga*), which will be mentioned below.

172 Karmay, *A Catalogue of Bonpo Publications*, 20. I modified the quote by using the English titles instead of the Tibetan ones.

173 Martin, *Mandala Cosmogony*, 29. He states on pp. 418-19 that the *Meditation Commentary* indicates this.

174 Reynolds, *The Threefold Practice of the Primordial State of the Mother Tantra*, 9. Martin also adds: "It seems that some missing parts were subsequently aurally revealed, by Dmu-ryal [Mushen Nyima Gyaltsen], which complicates matters still a bit more." D. Martin, electronic correspondence, November 1998.

175 Miluk Samlek, *Ma rgyud thugs rje nyi ma'i rgyud skor*, ed. Tshultrim Tashi (Dolanji, India: Tibetan Bonpo Monastic Community, 1985).

176 Ibid., index page. As for the contents of each of the chapters of the 1971 edition, see Karmay, *A Catalogue of Bonpo Publications*, 19-21. Below I will provide a brief summary of it as well, and later, the structure according to the 1985 edition. Since there is nothing said about Zhonu not having copied the brief commentary, it could be that it is included in the medium-length one.

177 Martin, *Mandala Cosmogony*, 13. In electronic correspondence (in November 1998), he confirmed that the historical preface (*bdu chad*) is "rather confusingly simply titled *sGom 'grel nyi ma'i snying po* in the version I originally used [the 1971 edition] (but then this title 'properly' belongs to a much larger collection of texts than just the preface)."

178 Karmay, *A Catalogue of Bonpo Publications*, 20; and Martin directs the reader to it as well. Martin, *Mandala Cosmogony*, 29.

179 Yongdzin Tenzin Namdak told me that *Meditation Commentary: Mandala of the Sun* includes the commentary on base and path. He is not sure about the commentary of the fruit since it no longer exists. Yongdzin Tenzin Namdak, telephone conversation, August 1998. Martin made clear to me that "when I

say 'Meditation Commentary' in this context, I mean nothing more than the historical preface [chap. 4 or *nga* depending on the edition]," and he added that "version G [the 1985 edition] is explicit about [that] initial text being a preface." D. Martin, electronic correspondences, November 1998. But as can be seen above, Martin affirms that the title "properly" encompasses "a much larger collection of texts than just the preface."

180 Yongdzin Tenzin Namdak, personal communication, Kathmandu, June 1997. Also see Reynolds, *The Mandala of the Sun*, 34.

181 Here is an instance in the Bön tradition where people are said to be not yet ripe to hear the teachings. This could be linked with the study of treasure discoveries in both traditions, as suggested above. Reynolds adds that there was one other yogi by the name of Buchi (*Bu ci*) that Guru Nontse considered ready for this teaching. Reynolds, *The Mandala of the Sun*, 34.

182 Martin, *Mandala Cosmogony*, 51.

183 G. Vico, *New Science* quoted in Martin, *Mandala Cosmogony*, 51.

184 Martin, *Mandala Cosmogony*, 51.

185 The text is *The Dhâraṇī of the Great Loving Mother, She Who Takes Care of Family Fears (Byams ma chen mo rigs kyi 'jigs skyobs ma'i gzungs)*. Martin, *Mandala Cosmogony*, 54.

186 Ibid., 52.

187 Ibid., 75.

188 Ibid., 54. Italics are mine.

189 Karmay, *A Catalogue of Bonpo Publications*, 20-21.

190 Ibid., 21.

191 *Mkhan chen nyi ma rgyal mtshan gyi gsang mchog gi dbang lung thob tshul*. For more information, see the entry for the text *The Three Basic [Secret] Mother Tantras with Commentaries* in the annotated bibliography in appendix 3.

192 Karmay, *A Catalogue of Bonpo Publications*, 21. Martin believes that Mushen Nyima Gyaltsen somehow received, and wrote down, the missing parts of the commentaries on the *Secret Mother Tantra*. This could also explain why it was included in the 1971 edition.

193 Yongdzin Tenzin Namdak told me during a conversation in his monastery in June 1997 that Zhonu was not a monk but a tantric practitioner, but this does not change the essence of the story.

194 Martin, *Mandala Cosmogony*, 31. The modification of the capital letter and the lack of hyphenation in the Tibetan transliteration, as well as the italics for the title are mine. Shardza Rinpoche's comments come from his *Legs bshad rin po che'i mdzod*, translated in Karmay, *The Treasury of Good Sayings*.

195 Martin, *Mandala Cosmogony*, 31.

196 It was not totally clear to me what Martin meant here by the "entire work"; did

he mean the whole of the *Commentary on the Base* (i.e., chapters *nga* to *na*), or just chapter *nga*? Fortunately, as noted above, he has since clarified that he meant solely chapter *nga*.

197 Martin, *Mandala Cosmogony*, 13.

198 Ibid. Thus, there are reasons to believe that Guru Nontse was more likely simply a redactor of, or an inspiration behind, the redaction.

199 On p. 29 of *Mandala Cosmogony*, Martin indicates that those include pp. 239–769, which would mean chapters *ca* to *'a*, but elsewhere (p. 13), he indicates that those start on p. 413, meaning chapter *pa* forward. The latter seems to be his position, although in either case, he attributes the chöd practice—as well as the other extant commentaries on the tantra of the path—to Milu Samlek.

200 The Tibetan calendar as we know it today began in the year 1027 BCE. Each year is associated with one of twelve animals and one of five elements. Each element rules for two years. *Rab 'byung* refers to the time it takes for each of the twelve animal-years to be combined with each of the five elements, making it a sixty-year cycle.

201 Martin, *Mandala Cosmogony*, 27.

202 Born in 1062 CE.

203 It might be argued that Milu Samlek never wrote the commentary on the fruit (and that is why it's missing). However, it is less plausible to argue that Milu Samlek never wrote the (missing) commentary on the chapter on the expedient use of death since it is the only one missing of the six chapters on the path of meditation, and is not even the last one (as is clear from the structure of the tantra as given below).

204 Even accepting a later chronology for Guru Nontse, this "remote past" need only be a little more than a century earlier in order to date the chöd of the *Secret Mother Tantra* before the *A dkar zhi gcod*. Of course if one accepts an earlier dating for Guru Nontse, there would be no need to pursue this historical examination—see (a) above.

205 Sun of Compassion (*Thugs rje nyi ma*) represents the name of the main deity: the King of Compassion (*Thugs rje rgyal po*) also called The Great Secret King (*gSang mchog rgyal po*) since he is included in the secret cycle. Yongdzin Tenzin Namdak, personal communication, Mexico, June 1998.

206 Martin claims that the three root texts of the secret mother tantras have these two different titles: a) *The Three Buddhahood Tantras (Sangs rgyas rgyud gsum)*, and b) *Compassion Sun [Sun of Compassion] (Thugs rje nyi ma)*. Martin, *Mandala Cosmogony*, 32. The change in capitalization and lack of hyphenation in Tibetan transliteration is mine. But according to Yongdzin Tenzin Namdak, these are not two different titles for this tantra, rather, like most Tibetan texts, one is the title and the other the subtitle or explanation of what the text contains.

207 For the list of the forty-five wisdom spheres, see Reynolds, *The Mother Tantra from the Bon Tradition*, 5-7.

208 In the Buddhist texts the truth dimension is *chos sku*, and the perfected or enjoyment dimension is *longs sku*.

209 According to Martin, the six principles of expediency are "only with some difficulty compared with the Six Dharmas of Nâropa." Martin, *Mandala Cosmogony*, 32–33. Chöd is not part of the six dharmas of Nâropa.

210 The path of seeing is the first ground (*sa, bhūmi*) of the path of a bodhisattva, the six parts of the path of meditation are the second to the seventh grounds, the path of freedom the eighth, the path of ripening the ninth, and the path of liberation the tenth.

211 Since there were no extant commentaries by Milu Samlek on the six parts of the fruit, no chapter enumeration is available, although the name and sequence follow the root text. Shardza Rinpoche wrote a commentary on the root text of the fruit entitled *Bras bu rdzogs sangs rgyas pa'i rgyud kyi dgomgs 'grel rnam par nges pa gsang ba mthar thug nyi zer drwa ba zhes bya ba bzhugs so.*

212 Reynolds, *The Mother Tantra from the Bon Tradition*, 6.

213 Note that this is the same text that Reynolds translates as *The Threefold Practice of the Primordial State of the Mother Tantra*.

214 Ibid., 17.

215 This survey comes from an index (*dkar chags*) composed by Geshe Lungrig Namgyal (to whom I am very grateful for providing this to me) and later explained by Yongdzin Tenzin Namdak Rinpoche. Taos, NM, July 1996. The index was reviewed again with Yongdzin Rinpoche in Kathmandu, June 1997. A copy of this index is in appendix 2.

216 Yongdzin Tenzin Namdak, personal communication, Kathmandu, June 1997, and later reiterated in Mexico, June 1998.

217 Lopon Tenpa'i Yungdrung, who now is the Khenpo or abbot of Tritsan Norbutse Monastery in Kathmandu, told me that if one does not realize the natural state, it is impossible to perceive things as illusory. In other words, when one is in the natural state, things are seen to be illusion, and one thus has no attachment toward them since one realizes their unreal nature. Lopon Tenpa'i Yungdrung, personal communication, Mexico, June 1998.

218 Here it functions as an antidote; if anger arises, one cultivates love and nails anger down with it. The same applies for the other afflictions.

219 It seems there is no conclusive argument regarding the right spelling of "Gyakhar Bachod." Martin (using the above spelling) translates it as "Chinese Fort Cattle Enclosure" (*Mandala Cosmogony*, 15), but also later as "Royal Fort" (*rgyal mkhar*) (*Mandala Cosmogony*, 66). Reynolds uses the latter, rendering it as the "Royal Citadel of Bachod" (*rGyal mkhar ba chod*). Reynolds, *The Threefold Practice of the Primordial State of the Mother Tantra*, 3.

220 Reynolds, *The Threefold Practice of the Primordial State of the Mother Tantra*, 6.

221 Ibid. I am not sure what Reynolds means by the austerities, but the total number of deities in this tantra is 366, and so maybe there is a relation there.

222 The last seven lineage holders prior to Mushen Nyima Gyaltsen are called the "seven excellent doctrine-holders" (*bar dar bdan 'dzin mchog bdun*), i.e., Guru Nontse up to and including the Zhangton Sonam pair. Yongdzin Tenzin Namdak, personal communication, Kathmandu, June 1997, reiterated in Mexico, June 1998.

223 This short lineage was compiled by analyzing Reynolds, *The Threefold Practice of the Primordial State of the Mother Tantra*, and *Mandala of the Sun*; as well as Martin, *Mandala Cosmogony*, together with personal communications with Yongdzin Tenzin Namdak. The main source of these is Shardza Rinpoche, quoted in Karmay, *The Treasury of Good Sayings*, 166–67. Shardza Tashi Gyaltsen is also part of the chain of this transmission. The *Secret Mother Tantra* commentaries themselves mention the lineage (Martin cites p. 205.4 of the 1971 edition), and Yongdzin Tenzin Namdak adds that the whole detailed long lineage through Lopon Sangye Tenzin is mentioned in the ritual text of the *Secret Mother Tantra*, the *Ma rgyud sgrub skor.*

224 Reynolds, *The Threefold Practice of the Primordial State of the Mother Tantra*, 9.

225 Yongdzin Tenzin Namdak, personal communication, Mexico, June 1998.

226 Śāntideva, *The Bodhicaryāvatāra*, trans. Kate Crosby and Andrew Skilton (New York: Oxford University Press, 1996), 34.

227 The six perfections are: giving (*sbyin pa*), ethics (*tshul khrims*), patience (*bzod pa*), effort (*rtsol ba*), meditation (*sgom pa*), and wisdom (*shes rab*).

228 Tonpa Shenrab taught the *Perfection of Insight* in brief, medium, and extended versions. He taught them in the god realm, in the human realm, and in the realm of the water serpentine beings (*klu, nāga*). Yongdzin Tenzin Namdak, telephone conversation, August 1998. The first-century Buddhist master Nāgārjuna (*kLu sgrub*) recovered them from the latter realm and later propagated them further in the human realm. However, Nāgārjuna recovered only a portion of the full corpus taught by Tonpa Shenrab: "The bonpos point out that their own Prajnaparamita collection (*khams gsum*) in sixteen volumes is much larger than the Indian Buddhist recension and, therefore, it is far more complete." Reynolds, *Yungdrung Bon, The Eternal Tradition*, 8. Martin also studied the problematic of the Tibetan transmission of the *Perfection of Insight*, and without claiming to be definitive, his conclusion was that "all evidence from close textual studies has shown that the 'transformations' [*bsgyur*, also 'translation'] went in the other direction [from what critics of Bön asserted],

from Bon to Chos." Martin, "The Emergence of Bon and the Tibetan Polemical Tradition," 109.

229 See Snellgrove, *The Nine Ways of Bon*, 136ff.

230 Reiko Ohnuma, "Dedhāna and the Buddhist Conceptions of the Body" (paper presented at the AAR, New Orleans, 1996), 161. This is derived from chapter 4 of her PhD dissertation.

231 Compare to Mumford who states: "the *gcod* [chöd] severance rite is said to carry the distribution to a higher plane by sharing out one's own body as a self-sacrifice." Mumford, *Himalayan Dialogue*, 162.

232 See Edou, *Machig Labdrön and the Foundations of Chöd*, 50–56.

233 Kalu Rinpoche, *Secret Buddhism: Vajrayāna Practices* (San Francisco: Clearpoint Press, 1995), 161, quoted in Harding, *Machik's Complete Explanation*, 49.

234 This way of practicing the four offerings is a traditional Bön custom that is common to all Bön monasteries, not just Tritsan Norbutse. Yongdzin Tenzin Namdak, telephone conversation, August 1998.

235 Snellgrove in *The Nine Ways of Bon*, translates "*A dkar theg pa*" as the "way of pure sound." As referred to earlier, its literal translation is the "way of the white A," where the white A is the primordial sound, or as Snellgrove renders it, the "pure sound."

236 Yongdzin Tenzin Namdak, telephone conversation, August 1998.

237 There are two schools of learning that a monk can follow in these monasteries. The majority follow the dialectic curriculum (*mtshan nyid*), which emphasizes scholarly understanding and debate; a small group follows the meditation curriculum (*sgrub grwa*). It is the monks following the latter who perform chöd among their practices.

238 The number of bowls can vary. Yongdzin Tenzin Namdak demonstrated the simplest way, which consists of placing one cup full of petals on top of a plate, and then pouring water on the cup. Also there are seven kinds of water offering texts that were composed and later rediscovered by different people. Yongdzin Tenzin Namdak, oral teachings, Jemez Springs, NM, July 1996.

239 Similar to the water offering, the burnt food offering has simpler and more elaborate versions, which depend on how big the fire is and the amount of food offered. Even though one always visualizes that the number of offerings is infinite and not limited to the actual number of physical offerings present, the quantity of physical offerings will be greater on special occasions, particularly if outside people are involved and bring their own offerings or donate money to purchase some. When performing a more tantric burnt food offering, bones are offered to appease anger, blood to satisfy desires, and meat to remove ignorance. Yongdzin Tenzin Namdak, oral teachings, Jemez Springs, NM, July 1996.

240 In the *Mother Tantra*'s main liturgy practice, "The Three Primordial Practices," referring to the lama, tutelary deity, and skygoer, there is a very brief offering of the body in the offering to the skygoer.

241 A lineage is said to be warm when it is temporally close to the receiver.

242 Yongdzin Tenzin Namdak and Tenzin Wangyal Rinpoche, among other Bönpo lamas, have taught it in this way to Westerners in India, Nepal, and the United States. (I have participated in a few of such teachings from 1995 to the present.) By the way the meditation-school followers in Nepal practice chöd, I infer that Yongdzin Tenzin Namdak taught it in that same fashion to them. Yongdzin Tenzin Namdak told me, however, that there are chöd practitioners that follow some of the other texts, in particular the *mKha' 'gro gsang gcod*. He mentioned a very serious such chöpa he knew, who lived in Dolpo, Nepal.

243 Rossi, "A Preliminary Survey of the *mKha' 'gro gSang gcod* teachings of Bon."

244 A particularly interesting point highlighted by Rossi is that the *Chöd of the Secret Skygoers* mentions the removal of the medical imbalances, which according to Tibetan medicine are imbalances of wind (*rlung*), bile (*mkhris pa*), and phlegm (*bad kan*). Ibid.

245 In the Buddhist chöd, the instruments are the same except for the bell, which has a different shape and is called *dril bu*. This is why the shang or silnyen is commonly called the Bönpo bell.

246 Other implements that can be used in the practice are a human skin (although Yongdzin Tenzin Namdak told me he had no proof of ever seeing a real one) or something that appears like one, and a hat (as seen in the cover photograph).

247 According to Yongdzin Tenzin Namdak, these implements were added to the chöd practice much later (maybe even as late as the eighteenth or nineteenth centuries). The Kashmiri Shaivites though, used a very similar kind of drum much earlier. Yongdzin Tenzin Namdak, personal communication, Kathmandu, June 1997. It is interesting to note that in the Buddhist chöd, Machig Labdrön is represented holding a damaru. I wonder if that was added later to her iconography or if she actually used one.

248 I received information on all three implements from Yongdzin Tenzin Namdak in New Mexico, July 1996. Here I will complement it with some material from Rinjing Dorje and Ter Ellingson, "Explanation of the Secret Gcod Damaru: An Exploration of Musical Instrument Symbolism," *Asian Music* 10, no. 2 (1979): 63–91.

249 Dorje and Ellingson in "Explanation of the Secret Gcod Damaru" claim that [at least in the Buddhist chöd] "the drum normally used is made of wood, [although] some texts suggest that a drum made from two human skulls may be used" (69). Later they state that the drum is "originally derived from an Indian prototype of the same name . . . made of two roughly hemispherical bodies

(either human skulls, the probable prototype, or wood)" (73). In any case, both do exist and, according to Yongdzin Tenzin Namdak, in the Bön tradition the ones made of skulls are preferred (if available).

250 Ibid., 73. I believe these characteristics enable one to play the appropriate sound for the corresponding offering. For Dorje's and Ellingson's exploration of the symbolism of the damaru, see ibid., 74–78.

251 I have no information about the composition of the alloy that is specified for the bell, although I have heard of specific alloys of other sacred objects such as a mirror (*me long*).

252 Sometimes other decorative motifs are used, such as for a stylized cloud.

253 Dorje and Ellingson, "Explanation of the Secret Gcod Damaru," 71.

254 Yongdzin Tenzin Namdak, for example, has one of leopard bone.

255 Dorje and Ellingson, "Explanation of the Secret Gcod Damaru," 71.

CONCLUSION

256 Yongdzin Tenzin Namdak, personal communication, Jemez Springs, NM, July 1995 and reaffirmed in Houston, June 1996.

257 Khetsun Sangpo Rinpoche, personal communication, Houston, March 1996.

258 Norbu, *The Dzogchen Ritual Practices*, 198.

259 Harding, *Machik's Complete Explanation*, 47.

260 Norbu, *The Dzogchen Ritual Practices*, 198. Diacritics were added.

261 Mumford, *Himalayan Dialogue*, 16.

262 Huber, "Putting the *gnas* Back into the *gnas-skor*," 52.

263 Mumford, *Himalayan Dialogue*, 164.

264 Reynolds, *Yungdrung Bon, The Eternal Tradition*, 4.

265 His Holiness the Fourteenth Dalai Lama of Tibet, "A Human Approach to World Peace," The Office of His Holiness the Dalai Lama, http://www.dalailama.com/page.62.htm.

266 Mumford, *Himalayan Dialogue*, 17. 'Heteroglossia' is a word coined by Bakhtin. In linguistics, it refers to the coexistence of distinct varieties within a single linguistic code. Bakhtin, and certainly Mumford, expand its meaning beyond linguistics into fields such as anthropology.

267 Savvas, "A Study of the Profound Path of *Gcod*," 82.

268 Harding, *Machik's Complete Explanation*, 16.

269 Dorje and Ellingson, "Explanation of the Secret Gcod Damaru," 65.

270 Huber, "Putting the *gnas* Back into the *gnas-skor*," 52.

271 Savvas, "A Study of the Profound Path of *Gcod*," 83. This was told to her by "the great gCod master the Venerable Zong Rinpoche" in a personal communication in India, 1980.

Epilogue

272 Martin, *Mandala Cosmogony*, 23.

273 Harding, *Machik's Complete Explanation*, 27. In fact, Harding discusses many interesting topics concerning the role of the female in Buddhist practice in general and how they apply to chöd, such as "woman or goddess," "motherhood," and others (see 21–34).

274 Mumford, *Himalayan Dialogue*, 208.

275 Martin, "On the Cultural Ecology of Sky Burial on the Himalayan Plateau," 365.

276 Stoddard, "Eat It Up or Throw It to the Dogs?"

APPENDIX I: *The Laughter of the Skygoers*

277 In the title of the text, *mkha' 'gro* is abbreviated to *'gro.*

278 In my master's thesis that is the basis of this book, I provided my own translation of this text. However, over the years, I have worked with others at Ligmincha Institute to create a unified version. So, as a way of cutting through part of my own ego and in order to create less confusion, I have decided to provide the Ligmincha translation here, which includes my work on it. However, I have added the Tibetan words, translations, and some footnotes for the book. A DVD of this chöd practice has recently been released in English, Spanish, and Polish (*Chöd Practice Demonstration*, Chamma Ling Productions, 2008).

279 To add clarity, the headings for the various parts of the sādhana are in bold.

280 *Sa trig yum; sa trig* is in the Zhang zhung language and signifies "insight" (*shes rab*). The complete name of this deity is *Sa trig er sangs*. P. Kvaerne says that the meaning of *er sangs* is not clear, although the equivalent in Tibetan, *sangs*, means "purified" or "clearing away" (see Kvaerne, *The Bon Religion of Tibet*, 25). Yongdzin Tenzin Namdak asserts that *er sangs* is the equivalent for *Byams ma* or "Loving Mother," therefore Satrig Ersang is the "Insight Loving Mother" (telephone conversation, July 1998).

281 *bsKal pa bzang mo*, the Mother of the Good Eon (i.e., the present time).

282 This part of the text is in the Zhang zhung language. The *dbu med* text reads *hri ho dzi ra da kki de pa ho*, where *de pa ho* is "homage" or "go for refuge," *hri ho* is "teacher" or "enlightened being," *dzi ra* is "tutelary deity," and *da kki*—which comes from the Sanskrit *ḍākinī*—is "skygoer." I have corrected the *dbu can* text accordingly in the translation that appears in this appendix.

283 *rGyal 'gong* are among the eight classes of hindering spirits. They are like foxes, not in appearance, but in that their mind is weak, they are easily frightened.

Therefore, the yogi's mind shocks them as a lion frightens a fox. This explanation was given to me by Yongdzin Tenzin Namdak, Mexico, June 1998. René de Nebesky-Wojkovitz says that the *rgyal 'gong* "are supposed to have been created by a union between the *rgyal po* and the *'gong po* [two of the eight classes of hindering spirits]. They seem to have retained some of the qualities of the former group, since they are said to reside in temples and monasteries." *Oracles and Demons of Tibet: The Cult and Iconography of the Tibetan Protective Deities.* Kathmandu: Tiwari's Pilgrims Book House, 300.

284 The khandros or skygoers invoked are: Totally Good Lady (*Kun tu bzang mo*), Perfection of Insight (*Shes rab phar phyin*), Wonderful Mother of the Luminous Lake (*Kye ma 'od mtsho*), Propitious Good Lady or Mother of the Good Eon (*bsKal pa bzang mo*), Compassionate Savior of All [beings] (*Thugs rje kun grol*), Luminous Blazing Sun (*'Od ldan nyi 'bar*), and Queen of Existence (*Srid pa'i rgyal mo*).

285 The six ornaments are: a five-skulled diadem, earrings, necklace, bracelets or anklets, sash, and waistband; all made of bones and skulls.

286 At this point, the practitioner is identified with Kalzang Ma.

287 I have corrected *zungs* to *zangs* in the *dbu can* text, on the basis of the *dbu med*. Yongdzin Tenzin Namdak states that even though *zangs* can mean "copper," in this context it means "vessel" in general without specifying any specific material it is made out of (personal communication, Mexico, June 1998). Three-thousand-fold is sometimes rendered as a billion since it is a thousand to the power of three, but I believe that it is helpful to retain the number three here, which alludes to the three realms (Tib. *khams gsum*, Skt. *tridhātu*) of desire (Tib. *'dod khams*, Skt. *kāmadhātu*), form (Tib. *gzugs khams*, Skt. *rūpadhātu*), and formless (Tib. *gzugs med khams*, Skt. *arūpyadhātu*).

288 Yongdzin Tenzin Namdak explains that *nar gyis* means melting down like syrup or honey (personal conversation, Mexico, June 1998).

289 The *A* at the navel is red and fiery, and it melts the upside-down white *HAM* that is at the crown of one's head.

290 "One hundred flavors" means for all possible tastes.

291 This is the offering to the four guests.

292 I have corrected *'chol* to *'cho*, in the *dbu can* text, on the basis of the *dbu med*. According to Yongdzin Tenzin Namdak, *'cho* means to "chew" or to "gnaw" (although I could not find it listed in any dictionary). *Lha rkang* means the inside of the bones, particularly the inside of the leg bones, although not to be confused with *rkang pa*, which means "leg." Yongdzin Tenzin Namdak, personal communication, Mexico, June 1998.

293 This is a unique Bön refuge, going for refuge to the four Yungdrung sources: the teachers (*bla ma*), the buddhas (*sangs rgyas*), the teachings (*bon*), and the

practitioners, specially the followers of Tonpa Shenrab (called *gshen rabs*), equivalent to bodhisattvas.

294 The *dbu can* indicates this line is part of the text, but it is clearly an annotation to the original *dbu med*.

295 Yongdzin Tenzin Namdak explained that the first kind of jewel is gold, the second silver, the third copper, and the fourth iron (personal communication, Mexico, June 1998).

296 The most common scarf offerings are called khata (*kha btags*), but here Shardza is being offered one of the special long silk khatas that are called lha dar.

APPENDIX III: *Annotated Bibliography of Chöd Texts from the Bön Tradition*

297 When Yongdzin Tenzin Namdak left Tibet, another Lopon was appointed at Menri Monastery. That Lopon made a handwritten copy of this text. When Yongdzin Rinpoche returned to Tibet in 1986, the Lopon who had made the copy of this text had already passed away, and someone else gave Yongdzin Rinpoche the handwritten copy.

298 According to the chronology of Nyima Tenzin (*Nyi ma bstan 'dzin*), the transmission was received in 1386 (see English preface of the text).

299 Edou states that Kyangtrul Namkha Gyaltsen was born in 1868. Edou, *Machig Labdrön and the Foundations of Chöd*, 225.

Printed in the United States
By Bookmasters